M000306168

Refining Me Still

Tidbits of Encouragement

Refining Me Still

Tidbits of Encouragement

Sonja Leet

Copyright

Unless otherwise noted, all scriptures referenced are from the King James Version of the Bible.

For permission requests, please write to the publisher, addressed "Attention: Permissions Coordinator," at the address below.

Printed in the United States of America

First Printing, 2020

ISBN: 978-1-951883-23-2

Cover Design by:

Editor: G.E.M.

Book Designer: Iris M. Williams

Butterfly Typeface Publishing
PO Box 56193
Little Rock AR 7215

www.butterflytypeface.com

Dedication

To Dad and Mom:

Thank you.

Table of Contents

Introduction 27
In His Presence 30
Best Time of Day 31
In His Presence 31
Nothing Like Being in His Presence 31
The Lord Is My Haven 31
The Holy Spirit's Constant Presence 32
God's Approachability 32
His Sovereignty 33
God Doesn't Promise an Easy Button 34
Trying to Put God in a Box 35
God's Sovereign Faithfulness 35
Trusting God's Sovereignty 36
God's Amazing Sovereignty 36
My Control or God's? 36
God Is God and I Am Not 37
God Is Still God 37
Our Limitless God! 37
Faith in a Sovereign God 38
All My Trust Is in God 38
Confidence in the Lord 38
Focusing on God's Purpose 39
Security in God's Sovereignty 39
Others 40
Loving Others as Christ Has Loved Me 41
Interacting with Others 41
Blessed to Be a Blessing 41
Forgiveness on a Deeper Level 42
We Are a Body of Believers 42
Faith and Love 43
Friends of Character 43
People 44

Risky Business 45
We Need Each Other 45
Influence...You Just Never Know! 46
Unity 46
People in Our Lives 47
Interconnected But Bringing Glory to God 47
We Need Each Other 47
Where God Wants Me to Be 48
Grace and Mercy to Others 48
What Does My Treatment of Others Reflect? 49
Trusting / Faith 50
Staying Strong 51
Faith 52
Resting 53
God's Sufficiency 53
Fully Dependent on God 53
Self Sufficient 54
God Knows 54
Joy 55
Trusting God or Trusting Myself? 55
God's Sometimes Unknown, But Perfect Timing 56
Faith 56
What Should I Fight For? 57
You Can Not Box in God 58
With God All Things Are Possible 59
Remember the Things God Has Done 59
True Trust Equals Rest 60
"Whoso Trusts in the Lord Happy Is He." 60
God's Faithfulness 60
Trusting Is Not Dependent on My Understanding 61
Still Trusting 61
Worrying or Trusting 61
Obedience and Trust 63

God is Always True to His Word ... 63
True Faith in God and Not Myself ... 63
Trusting the Lord Even with the Weather ... 63
Trusting Still ... 64
Trusting Means Letting Go ... 64
Faith in God that Leads to Action ... 65
Trusting God Rather Than the Media ... 66
God's Faithfulness ... 66
Choosing to Rest and Trust in the Lord ... 66
Hope and Trust in the Lord ... 67
I Can Always Trust the Lord ... 67
Spiritual Growth / Health ... 68
Vitamins or Medicine? ... 69
Change ... 69
God or a Roaring Lion? ... 70
Growth in the New Year ... 71
Learning? ... 72
In a Spiritual Battle ... 73
Physical and Spiritual Growth Take Time ... 73
Whose Power Am I Looking At? ... 74
Growth ... 74
Refining ... 74
Time with the Lord Produces Christ Likeness ... 75
Focus on God's Strength ... 76
Spiritual Strength ... 76
The Learning Times ... 77
Spiritual Battle ... 77
Words ... 78
Caring or Constructive Criticism? ... 79
My Words ... 79
Do I Always Need to Speak My Mind? ... 79
What Do My Words 'Taste' Like? ... 80
The Effect of My Words ... 81

The Flavor of Words 81

Guarding Our Words 82

Encourage Rather Than Discourage 82

Words 82

No Excusing Unkindness 83

Mercy and Grace 84

Grace 85

Mercy and Grace 85

God's Grace and Patience 86

Understanding I Am Not Worthy of Mercy 86

God's Mercy 86

Showing Mercy 87

God's Mercy 87

Mercy and Forgiveness 87

God's Grace and Mercy 88

Mercy and Grace Do Not Mean God Is Ignoring Sin 88

Grace vs. Works 89

The Love of God 90

Easter–i.e. love in action! 91

Weariness 92

Valentine's Day <3 92

The Love of God 93

God's Unconditional Love 94

Marriage-a Picture of God's Love for Me 94

To Grasp God's Love 94

God's Love, Greater Than Any Other 94

The Love of the Lord-- Valentine's Day 95

No Fear in the Love God Has for Us 95

Jesus Loves Me 96

God's Love for Me 96

Perfect Love Casts Out Fear 96

God Is God and Still Loves Me! 97

God's Love for Me 97

.... 98
Love for God & Others 98
The Greatest 2 Commandments 99
Indulge Me 100
I Love and the Holy Spirit Fixes 101
Love & Submission........ 101
Taking Time and Effort to Love the Lord More! 102
Serving the Lord Because I Love Him........ 102
The 2 Greatest Commandments 102
Love Produces Actions 103
Loved in Order to Love 103
The Impact of God's Commands 103
Loving the Lord 104
Surrender 105
To Be Still or Not to Be... 106
Releasing the Burden... 106
Comfort Zones........ 107
King? 108
Who is Leading? 108
Burdens 109
Surrender Day In & Day Out........ 110
Christ Our Perfect Example........ 110
Daily Surrender........ 110
Surrendering My Cares to the Lord 111
God's Ways or Mine?........ 111
Choosing to Let Go and Let God........ 112
Letting Go Is Sometimes Necessary........ 112
Casting Our Anxieties on Him........ 113
Beauty 114
Beauty........ 115
Where Does True Beauty Lie?........ 116
Let the Beauty of Jesus be Seen in Me 116
Beautiful Spirit? Beautiful Face? 117

Inner Beauty Vs. Outward Beauty 117
Beautiful in God's Eyes 117
The Beauty of Jesus Seen in Me 118
Focus 119
Choices 120
Thoughts Fixed on the Lord 120
Focus 120
Hazards of Multitasking 121
Focusing on God's Goodness and Power 121
Where Are My Energies Focused? 122
My Heart Is Fixed 122
God's Character 123
Focus on God's Character Alone 123
God's Amazing Creation 123
The Blesser or the Blessing? 124
Keeping My Focus on the Lord 124
No Complacency 124
More Is Not Necessarily Better 124
Distractions Anyone? 125
Praise 126
Praise 127
Past and Present 128
Amazing! 129
Counting Blessings 129
Rejoicing 130
Praise 130
Who Am I Praising? 130
A Grateful Heart vs. A Whining Spirit 131
The Goal of Praise 131
Praising the Lord--Obviously 132
God Is Still Faithful and I Need to Be Grateful 133
Quicker to Share God's Praise! 133
What Praising God Is Not 133

Looking for God's Blessings and Praising Him for Them 134
Thankfulness Rather Than Complaining 135
Praising the Lord Needs to Be More the Norm 135
God on the Throne of My Life 136
.... 137
Reflecting God The Father, Son, And Holy Ghost 137
"2012" 138
Examples 138
What Kind of Infuser? 139
Truth Does Not Change 140
Reflecting Christ Rather Than Self 141
Time with God Changes Perspective 141
Encouraging? 142
Receiving Generosity Should Result in Being Generous 142
A Man After God's Own Heart 142
Thankfulness 143
All About Perspective 143
All Things Pleasing to the Lord 144
Influence? 144
What Kind of Tone Setter Am I? 144
Reflecting Christ 144
Infused with God 145
God Is the One Who Needs to be Seen Not Me 145
More Like Jesus 145
Reflecting Christ 146
Bringing Glory to God 146
What Does My Walk Look Like? 146
Glorifying God 146
I Belong to Jesus, Am I Living for Him? 147
.... 149
What is On My Mind? 149
Adjusting My Attitude 150
Actively Taking Thoughts Captive 150

God’s Perspective ... 150
Controlling Thoughts ... 151
"What's on Your Mind?" ... 151
What Am I Feeding My Mind? ... 151
Pondering the Goodness of God ... 152
Variety...Good or Bad? ... 152
... 153
His Blessings ... 153
Excelling at Thankfulness ... 154
A Good Day ... 155
God...Our Best Source (for 2013) ... 155
Gifts ... 156
Declaring God’s Working ... 157
Blessings ... 158
The Blessing of Trials ... 158
God’s Generosity ... 159
God’s Blessings/ Peace ... 159
God’s Blessings ... 159
Blesser and Deliverer ... 160
Aware of God’s Blessings ... 160
Blessing of God’s Word in My Language ... 160
Paying Attention to God’s Goodness ... 161
Seeing the Blessings When I am Willing to Look ... 161
Living in the “Now” ... 162
Prayer ... 163
Hopeful or Worrisome? ... 164
Praying in Faith ... 165
Pray-Yes, Worry-No ... 165
Importance of Prayer ... 165
A Sweet Sound in God’s Ears ... 165
Diligent in Prayer and Trusting the Lord ... 166
... 167
His Ways and Purpose ... 167

Is Friction Always Bad? 168
Why?? 169
When Life Changes... 171
God's Ways vs. Man's Ways 172
Paths 173
Who Am I Fighting? 173
Life Like a Puzzle 174
God's Plan for Me 175
Timing 175
Spiritual Gifts 175
God's Yoke Not Mine 176
Distraction vs Purpose 176
Content in Who God Made Me to Be 177
God Has a Plan 177
His Time and His Ways 178
It's All About Him! Not Me 178
Learning God's Ways Are Better 178
God's Purpose Is Always Good 179
God's Perfect 'Puzzle Piecing' 179
God's Ways Are Amazing 179
God Does Not Always Use Those That We Would Think 180
The Lord's Leading 180
God's Timing 181
.... 182
Wisdom 182
True Wisdom Comes from God 183
True Wisdom 183
Wisdom and Other Things of Lasting Value 183
Different Forms of Wisdom 184
Wisdom Is 184
Wisdom Is Greater Than Riches 185
Asking for God's Wisdom 185
Always Seeking God's Wisdom 185

Godly Wisdom 186
Help 187
Abundantly Available 188
My Help Comes from the Lord, Maker of Heaven and Earth 189
My Help Comes from God 189
Who Am I Counting on to Win My Battles? 190
God's Faithfulness 190
Hope 191
Sweeter 192
Hope 193
Hope Requires Waiting 194
Hoping in God 194
True Hope Is in God's Word 195
Scripture 196
The Beauty of Scripture 197
Loving the Flavors of God's Word 198
The Treasure of God's Word 198
So Much in Scripture! 198
Obedience 200
Whose Idea of Greatness? 201
Quick to Listen 201
God's Ways Vs. Man's Ways 203
He Already Knew 204
Obedience–Not a Bad Word 204
Not Giving into Sin 205
My Responsibilities? 205
Yielded to the Holy Spirit's Working in Me? 206
Obedience to God 206
Pliable in God's Refining Process 207
Total Obedience Means No Questions Asked 207
Obedient in Spite of the Struggles 207
Obedience 208
Listening to Him and Not Me 208

Diligence in Obedience 208
.... 210
His Faithfulness 210
Still... 211
Repetition 211
God's Reliability 212
What if God Reacted/ Responded Like We Do? 212
God is My Best Source for All Things! 212
Lifetime of Construction--But Not Excuses 213
Resting in God 214
God Over ALL 214
Perfect Hearted, and God Over All! 214
God Is True to Himself 215
God's Character 215
Only God Can Change Hearts 215
God is Always Working 216
Resting in God's Care 216
The New Year 216
.... 217
His Peace 217
Peace and Rest 218
Stillness Brings Rest 218
Content and At Peace 218
Listening to the Lord, Rather Than Myself 219
.... 220
His Power 220
Wimpy or Strong? 221
Where Does My Help Come From? 221
Problems 222
So God Can Receive the Glory 223
Far Reaching Power of God 224
God Is Greater 224
What I Can't Handle, God Can 224

God's Ability Trumps My Inability! 225

God's Power -Beyond! 225

.... 226

Christmas 226

Christmas Spirit 227

Christmas Distractions 228

.... 229

His Parenting 229

Fear 230

God-the Perfect Father 231

Parenting 232

God, the Better Parent 233

Belonging to Him 233

Understanding God's 'Parenting' 233

God Is in Every Part of My Life 234

Boundaries Are a Good Thing 234

Precious in His Sight 235

Salvation 236

The Gift of Salvation 237

Christ's Payment for Our Sin 237

Easter Victory Before Earthly Worries 237

Sin Covered Completely! 238

.... 239

Sin 239

All Sin, Seen and Unseen Has an Effect 240

Idols in Our Lives? 240

Dealing with Our Own Sins 242

My Sin Is Never Justified 242

Patience/ Impatience 243

Soaring Like Eagles 244

Impatient Much? 245

More Focus on the Product Than the Time Frame 245

The Benefits of Waiting 246

God's Patience Should Impact Mine 246

What Can I Do For Him? 247

.... 247

Deliberately Following 248

Giving Back 248

Giving 249

What Can I Do for Him? 250

Doing All for God 250

Glory in God, Not Mankind 250

Pure Before the Lord 251

Pleasing or Wearying God 251

Worship Can Be Done Anywhere! 251

Time Given to God 252

As Loyal to God as I Am to Others? 252

Faithful to Him! 252

I Belong to the Lord 253

What Does God See? 255

Foreword

I have been friends with Sonja Anderson Leet for over 35 years. She's been one of the few people I have remained in contact with from that era of my life that knows me well enough to love me in SPITE of myself! If it weren't for her constant efforts at making contact, we would probably have lost touch completely when my husband was stationed in the Philippines while in the Air Force during the early 90's. I'm so glad she made the effort! She has enriched my life in many ways, not the least of which is holding me accountable and being my favorite prayer warrior!

That's who my friend is.

Sonja is loyal to family and friends, loves her husband, children and grandchildren with all her heart - almost to a fault, sometimes - and loves God with even more fervor (Love ya, Sonja 😊).

This book is her heart on paper. Not only is she constantly learning, but she is consistently teaching what she learns by putting those lessons down on paper (or computer screen) to share with those whom she cares about. I love reading her thoughts as she writes regarding what the Lord is teaching her that day. I have been following her writings for several years and am always amazed at how she can articulate in a way that makes it seem simple, though she is very clear that life's lessons are NOT always as simple as they seem, nor are they as complicated as we try to make them.

I love Sonja's openness to the Lord's leading, her transparency when sharing and her willingness to admit that sometimes she has difficulty in the following, just like everyone else. God has given her a talent and a gift that I, for one, am so glad she is willing to use to the glory of God. Seeing life with His perspective is difficult at the best of times, but Sonja always manages to bring it around to exactly that…HIS PERSPECTIVE.

When I'm having a difficult time, she is always the first one to help me see my situation in a different light and pray with me to let the Lord be seen through me, not just in spite of me. She shows that ability in her writings.

I am sure you will be blessed, challenged and uplifted by Sonja's thoughts in this devotional book. Learn to look at daily situations through Jesus' eyes; let the Holy Spirit show you some insight about the mind of God the Father through her writings and be challenged to seek Him in YOUR daily walk.

I believe Sonja's practicality will lead you to view your life situations through God's filter…after all, isn't that what we need… A clearer vision of how God wants us to be through His Word?

This collection of devotional thoughts will assist in just that way.

Enjoy – I know I have, several times over! ☺

Affectionately,

Debra Salzman

Friend and Sister in Christ

Acknowledgments

Dad and Mom, thank you for all that you taught me about the Lord as i was growing up, i thank you!

Thank you for not just teaching me the facts of God's Word, but also living them out.

Thank you for teaching me the Gospel, so that i would one day put my faith and trust in the Lord Jesus Christ!

Thank you for always referring me back to God's word when i had struggles and hardships and for encouraging me to be whatever the Lord wanted me to be and do! And for the prayers you offer on my behalf, as well as for my husband, children and grandchildren, i thank you!!

I love you and am so thankful for your love and prayers over all my years!

To God be the glory and praise for you!!

In Loving Gratitude,

Sonja

Introduction

Listening and learning.

This writing experience was new to me. During the process, I was reminded that there is always something new to learn – no matter the age. There is no need to be afraid because the Lord is in charge. He does go before us and prepare the way. No matter where or when, He still leads.

Allowing the Lord to lead doesn't mean there won't be struggles with fear or worry.

Trust in the Father's heart (because it is always trustworthy) and in the right perspective and realize that life is for His purpose and not our own.

During my times of meditation, I learned to listen for the still small voice of God. Learning to listen for God is just as important as responding. Waiting on God's response is the key to prayer and meditation.

It is my desire and prayer that just as He has impressed on my heart to write these 'tidbits of encouragement,' they will be used for His intent and not mine.

May He bless and challenge each of you (my readers) in ways that only He knows is needed and that you will see His hand in your lives!

A Note From The Author

Please read!

Throughout this body of work, you will consistently see the letter I printed in lower case. This is intentional. It will be capitalized at the beginning of a sentence, but other than that it will be printed as "i" to remind me of who "i" am in comparison to God. God is so much greater!

The publisher was also instructed to edit the work so that it was as if I were talking directly to you – conversational style.

Please enjoy,

Sonja Leet

In His Presence

Best Time of Day

Thinking this morning that my time with the Lord each morning, Bible and journal in my lap, is the best part of my day! It is where i am most comfortable and at peace. It is about taking time to listen, meditate and talk with my Lord!! But i also want always to remember that this is not time with a peer, this is time spent with Holy God!!...we are not even close to equal!!

In His Presence

Thinking that no matter where i may be physically, i want to be most "at home" with my Lord!! Not like He is my peer because He is God!! But being content and exactly where i want to be in His presence!

Nothing Like Being in His Presence

I was reading this morning about dwelling in the Lord...To dwell means to abide or sit down, to stay. And i think about how sweet it is to spend time with Jesus! How sweet to be in His presence all the time! The more i make a point to think on Him and who He is, the better i will know Him and His character, and the more i will love that there is nowhere i can go and He not be there! There is rest, and peace, and joy, in His presence!! There is absolutely nothing like it!!

The Lord Is My Haven

Thinking about the fact that the Lord is my haven-- He is peace. He is a safe place. He brings contentment and safety! No matter whether there is a 'storm' in my life, or not! To be at His side is always a wonderful place to be!

The Holy Spirit's Constant Presence

As i read about David dancing before the Lord, because they were bringing the Ark of the Covenant back to the children of Israel...my thoughts go to the fact that this was a symbol of God's presence among them. It wasn't a miracle as such, but the thought of God's presence caused King David to dance! And it makes me do a bit of a self-check--am i excited, at the very least, extremely grateful for the fact, that as a Christian, the Holy Spirit lives within me and is present with me always...it really IS amazing that He is with me no matter what or where I am!! I am so thankful that He loves me to such an awesome degree!!...to think of spending every day with your best friend, how great would that be! And yet this is even better!!

God's Approachability

Thinking this morning about how blessed i am by the sweet relationships and friendships i have. But there is none quite so sweet as the relationship that the Lord offers, through His Son!! What an amazing love that never fails and never ends!!! Why would i not want to be a part of that?! As i was thinking about the fact that God is Almighty, and Most High, this morning, i got to thinking about people who are of rank and status here on this earth. They are UN-approachable, and Un-reachable! But the God of the universe wants me to talk to Him, and confide in Him, and He really does deserve all praise and glory! He has every right to push us away (especially seeing He knows all about us, the good and the bad), and yet He doesn't! He offers everlasting life and a closeness with Himself!! Amazing Love!!!! So far beyond our wildest dreams!!

His Sovereignty

God Doesn't Promise an Easy Button

In 1993 our family moved to Fayetteville, NC. We were positive that the Lord wanted us here. Though *absolutely nothing*, and i do mean nothing, went as we had planned. After being here a few months, i remember having a discussion with my husband as to whether or not we should have moved. But as we talked and discussed things, we were reminded that nothing was a surprise to God! He knew exactly how everything was going to happen and work out (or not). And still He made it quite clear that we were to move here. I am afraid that at times, we think that if God really wants us to do something, it should be easy. Because we live in America– where we have our own homes, and computers, and cars, and most of the time, most of the things we want (though if we were honest, don't really need). We have things so easy, and so easily accessible: running water, modern plumbing, communication devices galore, entertainment, and the list goes on! We have soooooooooooo much!! Really, we do!! But God *never* says follow me and everything will be easy. He doesn't!! Actually, He says we will suffer persecution and be hated by the world, like He was and is. What He does promise, is that when we follow Him, He will get us through the hard times. He will be our strength, especially when we are weak! He promises to never leave us or forsake us! But never does He promise a life with no problems or challenges. There are so many things that we will put our efforts into... whether we pray about them or not...bodily strength, smaller physique, job promotions, daily jobs, and the list goes in different directions, for each of us. But the point is that we will do those sorts of things and *work hard in spite of opposition.* But when it comes to something the Lord makes clear that He wants us to do, we get wimpy and decide that it must not be what He wanted, after all, because it doesn't come together the way we thought it would or should. I was thinking about this sort of thing recently and realized that so many times when that happens, it is because the Lord wants HIS glory, and power, and ability, to be seen!! Not mine, Not yours, but HIS! Oh, that i will have the mind of Christ, rather than my own! His ways are perfect, and His counsel will never lead me astray! But i must be sure to be in His Word, and seeking His guidance, so that i will know what His will is.

Trying to Put God in a Box

Often i think of us, as trying to put God 'in a box'–wanting Him to do things, *our* way, and in *our* time (or even *doubting* that He is able to do something, because *we* can't understand how it could ever come about). But as i was reading today in 1 Kings, Solomon was praising God, and speaking about how the heavens and earth cannot contain Him!! And it made me grasp better just how amazing and marvelous that is!! That the problems, and cares of this world, (the things that seem to be so confining to us) are powerless against God Almighty!!! Even the hearts of mankind...no matter what they may look like to you and me, are fully within God's capability to change! So...be encouraged!! God is NOT "in a box"!! And there is always hope in the Lord, who is able to do all things well!!

God's Sovereign Faithfulness

God is sovereign -- something I know to be true! I know because of people we read about in the Bible, and how God used anything, and everything, to work things according to His good plan. I also know because of personal experience and watching Him work in the lives of others i know. But as i ponder this, i realize that while i am quick to speak it, sometimes i am not as quick to remind myself, when i start to worry or overthink things. I want to be so in tune to, and with my Lord, that not only is it the first thing to come out of my mouth, but it is also the first thing that pops into my mind-- that God IS sovereign, and He IS faithful always!! Thank You, Lord!!

Trusting God's Sovereignty

Pondering God's sovereignty this morning...the fact that He is in control of all things, I don't completely comprehend it, but i AM to trust it! I must admit that i don't always do that like i should. But the truth is, that He is trustworthy, in every way!! There is not a detail that He forgets, or misses, no matter how big, or small it may seem to me. There is never a cause to worry or to stress, only to trust and rest and rely on Him!!! In ALL things!

God's Amazing Sovereignty

Thinking that to trust the sovereignty of God, is not to be complacent, but rather to be trusting, and resting, in all things. After all, to be sovereign is to be in control of all things-- not just some, or just sort of, in control. My Heavenly Father is AMAZING!! And i am pondering whether i live that way all the time...

My Control or God's?

I am thinking about the act of trusting, today. God is faithful and always dependable! And He is in total control. Not me! There was a specific time in my life, that i realized how much i wanted to control things. And God really worked on me for about a year. But every so often, i realize those control issues come up in ways, that i may not realize...if i am worrying, it is because i would like to be able to control whatever situation might be at hand, at the time. If i am stressing, or overthinking things, or wondering about all the 'what if's' ...those are all things that are a result of me wanting control, and not having it. But, only God is always in control. And only He can be trusted all the time! The truth is that if i am willing to trust Him completely (more than i trust myself), then there will be peace! And truly, there is nothing like the peace that the Lord gives when i surrender all my anxieties and control issues into His hands! I am responsible for my actions, but sometimes i just need to rest in the Lord, trusting that He will be exactly who He says He is!

God Is God and I Am Not

I am thankful today that the Lord is always true to His word and in total control. Sometimes, i am afraid we get disgruntled with the way He does things. But the truth is that He is God, and i am not! I really am glad for that, because if i knew all He knows and had the control He does, i would definitely mess things up! Just my pondering thoughts today...

God Is Still God

Numerous thoughts on my mind this morning.... but i am impressed that when i look at the goings on around the world, i can either get all in a panic, or I can choose to rest in the fact that God has not lost control, and He always takes care of His children. The choice is mine...i can panic and stress, or i can trust and rest.

Our Limitless God!

Pondering numerous things this morning...but i feel led to share something that i was actually thinking on last week. I was reading in 1 Kings 8, as Solomon is dedicating the temple. Verse 23,27 say, " And he [Solomon] said, LORD God of Israel, there is no God like Thee, in heaven above, or earth beneath, who keeps covenant and mercy with Thy servants who walk before Thee with all their heart:...But will God indeed dwell on the earth? Behold, the heaven and heaven of heavens cannot contain Thee: how much less this house that I have built?" Way too often, i am afraid we limit our trust and faith in God? We- at least i - can have a tendency to box Him in, as though He has to work within my understanding or imaginations. But the truth is, that He is beyond my every imagination! His ways and abilities are so great! They, like Him, cannot be contained!! We belong to and serve a Limitless God!!!!

Faith in a Sovereign God

Without faith it is impossible to please the Lord...and i am thinking i need to remember that in all things...big or small, important or seemingly not...God is sovereign in it all!! And He wants me to know that He rewards those who diligently seek Him! It is evident that He means Himself--not necessarily stuff, or answers, but Him...hmm...my morning pondering...

All My Trust Is in God

Pondering the truth that God has not given us the spirit of fear, but of power, and of love, and of a sound mind! There are many things in this world that can cause me to fear if my focus is not on the Lord. But He desires for me to put all my trust and hope in Him! And it IS safely placed there-- now and always!! Only resting in Him will bring true peace and contentment...

Confidence in the Lord

Putting my confidence in the Lord does not mean i always see Him do what i want or expect Him to do. It does mean however, that i trust Him, and keep on obeying. I may be caught off guard, but He never is! When He asks me to do something, He already knows all the details, I'm hoping that what the Lord is teaching me, will somehow encourage you today.

Focusing on God's Purpose

Wanting to focus on reverencing and trusting the Lord.... rather than focusing on this world, and the things in it, God is sovereign over all! That includes: the things i do and don't have, the way i do or don't look, the weather, the changes that happen on a daily basis, and how my life is, compared to someone else's. The list can grow quite long. But all in all, i am here for His purpose, and not my own...i am pretty sure i need to be reminded of that, often!

Security in God's Sovereignty

I am so glad that the Lord is over ALL, the big, the small, and everything in between!! Nothing catches Him off guard. He goes before me and prepares the way! That means i can rest in Him! He gives me free will, but also knows when i need to be 'reined' in. I am so thankful that He is my Savior and Lord!!

Others

Loving Others as Christ Has Loved Me

"This is my [Jesus'] commandment, "That ye love one another as I have loved you...These things I command you, that ye love one another." John 15:12,17 At first, i just read this and think 'ok' but i am to love others as God loves me!! Not something i need to slide past, but really consider to what extent that requires me to be loving! Much to ponder...

Interacting with Others

Thinking that God has given spiritual gifts and abilities, in order for His children to encourage each other and to help us to grow. But in order for that to work we must interact with one another. And that is not just a "hello" on Sunday...we give so much effort to things and stuff, but how much time do we give to each other...just my morning ponderings...

"Let your speech always be gracious, seasoned with salt,
so that you may know how to answer each person."
Colossians 3:16 (ESV)

Blessed to Be a Blessing

Thinking this morning that the Lord blesses me to be a blessing. He never intends to bless any of His children only to have those blessings stop with them. They are meant to share, no matter what form they may come in. It makes me think of the difference between a pond and a river. In a pond, the water just sits there and gets stagnant, but a river runs, and the water is usually good to drink. Anyway, here is to a day of being a blessing to someone else because of the amazing ways the Lord has blessed me! Have a happy day!

Forgiveness on a Deeper Level

"Hatred stirs up strife, but love covers all sins." Another word for strife is quarrels. And as I read this verse, I naturally think about forgiveness. But the Holy Spirit brings to mind that I need to see what the word "covers" means in the original language. And how practical it becomes, when I see that it means, to pardon. So I am still thinking forgiveness... and it is, but... to pardon means to lift the penalty or to no longer penalize! Wow, it is like a light bulb of practicality came on! If I am going to say, I love someone, whether it is my spouse, a family member, or a friend, then when I have a quarrel (disagreement) with them, or am at odds with them, not only do I need to forgive them, but I need not to hold a grudge, hang it over their heads, or bring it back up...because that is penalizing them... Hmm...

Thinking about how our lives always impact those around us, whether we want them to or not...wanting my life to shine Christ!!

We Are a Body of Believers

I love that the Lord makes us a family of believers, that He wants us to be connected to Him first and foremost, and that He desires us to interact with each other! Whether we have a close relationship, one that is just starting, or one that is somewhere in between there, God didn't intend for us to be loners or by ourselves. We need each other to encourage, to hold accountable, and to be there for each other because we are to be like Christ! He is always here for us!

Faith and Love

Faith in the Lord and love for people…those are the things the Lord laid on my heart this morning. And i thought, okay? Those are good things. But as i have pondered on those things, throughout the day, there becomes a deeper understanding. At times, i can look at others, their actions, or attitudes can be rather frustrating to me. Why won't they just_______? It would be so much easier! But then, i come back to those phrases, to have faith in the Lord, and to have love for people. Could it be that my faith is not fully in the Lord? I hate the thought of that, but the truth is, that at times, my faith is either in myself and what i can do to help people be what they need to be, or i think, if they would just put themselves in this circumstance, or…or…or…my dear friend, (you know who you are ;)) tells me, "Sonja, you are overthinking it!" That is her sweet way of redirecting my thoughts off of trusting myself and my own ways, back to trusting the Lord ;). I would want others to see me and to see a work in progress. And with that view, they would be patient with me, love me along the way, and trust the Lord to work in me, as only He can, and in His perfect way and time! Ohhh ;) yes, that is what i need to be doing as well. I need to trust the Lord to do a work, not only in me, but also in the lives of others i love and may be burdened for. After all, they don't belong to me; they belong to Him! I am called to love them like Jesus loves me, and to be patient because, they too, are a work in progress! I am finding that praying for someone is an amazing way for me to redirect my focus on God and His ability! I have never had anyone turn me down when i tell them i will pray for them. ;) My hope is in the Lord!

Friends of Character

As i read this morning about Mephibosheth, i am thinking about the things that "could have been" for him. He was the grandson of King Saul, son of Jonathan (King David's best friend). But he was injured when his nurse dropped him, many years before. His dad and grandfather were both dead–in fact most, if not all, of his family was gone. King David had called for him, many years later, to come live with him, in his house. Mephibosheth could have acted as though he was entitled. He could have been bitter because all of it could have been his, if things had gone differently. But he never was! And when it came to loyalty to the king, he was always loyal, even when others were not. I am inspired by his character! Thinking that, not only was he a good subject, but he was also a good friend. Don't we all want good friends, friends who are loyal, humble, and honest? I do!...but, i am also challenged that i need to be a good friend and that i need not only to say i belong to Christ, but that my life needs to be reflective of Him! Maybe there is someone specific today that the Lord wants me to connect with or maybe that He wants you to connect with, someone who needs to see Christ's character in our lives. :-) Oh, to be His minister, no matter what! May you be a blessing to others and blessed as well! :-)

People

I am thinking about the people in my life today...My husband, and 'kids' (though they are grown), my family and friends, and acquaintances, as well as those who have created challenges in my life and have given me opportunity to exercise grace. ;) There are teachers, preachers, and others i look up to and those who i wish i could look up to, but really just need to pray for. There are those who are easy to love and those who are a little more work, those who i wish i could see every day and those i will not see until i reach Heaven, someday. But all of them, the Lord has blessed my life with because as easy as they might be to love, or as challenging as it has been, the Lord has a reason for them to be in my life. And since His plans are always for my good and His glory, they are all a part of His blessings on me! Now, the next time i am having a hard time with someone, i can come back to this and remind myself of what i know to be true. ;-) May you all be blessed with all the people in your life that you need, in order to become more like our Saviour!

Risky Business

As i was reading in my Bible this morning, i came across a couple of verses that talked about how Paul and others, had poured themselves into the lives of the people, at Thessolonica. They not only preached the gospel, but really let the people there know who they really were. They allowed themselves to be vulnerable. And it makes me think about how risky it can seem, at times, to put myself "out there." What if people don't like me? What if i do all kinds of things, make all kinds of efforts, and they don't respond at all, or in a way that says, "Leave me alone"? I don't want to be rejected. But then i think of Christ! My perfect example! The One i am supposed to reflect in my daily life...and the little phrase, "What would Jesus do?" comes to mind! He gave of Himself, on behalf of others, all the time, people who would use Him, and eventually crucify Him! He knew that all along!! And He gave anyway!! Yes, it can seem a bit risky. But if it means someone else may see Christ in me, and be encouraged, or drawn to Christ, is it not worth it?? Oh, that i would not shy away from truly loving people, because of fear! But that i will let the Lord have full sway in my life and be sensitive to His leading me to "put myself out there", so that others will see HIM!!

We Need Each Other

God's word supports the fact that we need each other. But to be able to do that, we have to allow ourselves to be vulnerable, as well as available. Thinking back to the sermon on Sunday about doing our part in the body of Christ, using the spiritual gifts God has given us, and also speaking the truth in love...to do that, i must be pliable in the leading, and directing of the Holy Spirit. But when we are there for each other we will be stronger!

Influence...You Just Never Know!

Sometimes i think that my range of influence is of little effect. The truth, however, is that none of us know how many people we affect. There is the whole thing also of a "domino effect"... We should never get the idea that what we do only affects us. I just finished reading the book of Ruth in my Bible. It is a short 4 chapters, but the people in this book are a part of the lineage that Christ was born into!!! It would be tempting to think, "What difference do these people make?", but we just never know!! It is so important to be yielded to Christ no matter what!!

Unity

It has been on my mind lately, that the devil is on a rampage to destroy the family. There are different ways, within different families. But if he can get our families to divide and be divisive, then he has a foothold to divide the church (the family of God). We work awful hard at things that have little value. But what about our homes? Are we fighting? Why? Are the things we fuss about really that important? People are so much more important than preferences. I have heard people say, "But i didn't get to pick my family"...and to that i would answer that God did. He put you with those people, for a very specific reason. I am burdened for our marriages, our homes, our church. If they start to fall apart, then there is a domino effect. In my opinion we are often fighting for the wrong things...praying today for our marriages, our homes, and our churches, that we would learn what it really means to have harmony and unity! (and that does often mean giving up my desires for someone else's--but holding no resentment about it)...just my thoughts/observations...

People in Our Lives

After reading this morning in 1 Samuel, about David and his friendship with Jonathan, as well as the fact that Saul wanted to kill him...i am impressed with the fact that i need to be thankful for all the people in my life--from those i thoroughly enjoy, to those that i struggle with a little bit...God has put them all in my life for a reason, and His reasons are always for my good!!

Interconnected But Bringing Glory to God

As i head to bed, i am thinking of all the people that the Lord has placed in my life...past and present. They have all affected me in some way or another. And likewise, i have done the same. God meant us to be inter-connected. It is part of His purpose and process to make us into who He wants us to be. It is a good thing, :) but i do not want to forget that, however i may impact you, or someone else, it is to be in such a way, that brings honor and glory to the Lord!

We Need Each Other

Thinking this morning about how independent we are NOT! If the power company workers, and the water company workers, and the gas company workers, and the traffic light manufacturers, and the road maintenance workers, and the_______ workers did not go to work, life would not be what we know it to be! Other people's' lives may not "seem" very important to us,(because they do not seem to directly affect us) but the truth is that they are important to God! And He knows why each one is where they are, doing what they are doing! And He has orchestrated it all! So thankful that He has!! And also so thankful that He has chosen to make each of you a part of my life in some way or another.

The more we spend time with God, the more we are ready to spend time with others.

Where God Wants Me to Be

As i was reading a portion of scripture in 1 Kings, this morning, i was reminded that as a child of the King, i am important! NOT because of me, but because i belong to the Lord!! And though my realm of influence may not seem very large, it is still significant, because it is where God has placed me! And these are the people who He wants to have an impact on me, and vice versa. All in all, i believe it is about being content to be where He has me, with whom He has me because it is all a part of His plan! And besides that, i can always trust the One who loves me more than anyone will ever love me!!

Thinking about the fact that i need to give thanks, and praise to the Lord for His goodness, whether He does things my way, or not. He is always good, no matter what!!

Grace and Mercy to Others

As i sit pondering this morning, i am reminded that the world is nice to those who are nice to them, and unkind to those who are unkind. But God calls His children to be different. We are called to be like Christ. And that means being gracious all the time. It means when someone makes me mad, i don't get back at them. It means if they are ugly to me, that i am not ugly in return...it is not always easy to respond in grace and mercy, but it is always right. For all the grace and mercy the Lord gives to His children on a daily basis, we can surely give it out in like manner...

What Does My Treatment of Others Reflect?

Pondering this morning...if the Lord treated me like i treat others, would i grasp how much He loves me? Is how i am treating others bringing Him glory? I'm not talking just about family or best friends, but anyone... It definitely is a guideline i should consider on a more regular basis...

Trusting / Faith

Staying Strong

Sometimes the Lord puts me in places where i am just trying to shine for Him and make a positive difference in the lives of others because i love Him. But honestly, sometimes i do grow weary and wonder when the difference will actually show. And i realize that that should put up a red flag to me because i am called to be obedient, not bring results (that is God's job). Trusting Him to use me in His way, and not my own, takes faith and patience. And sometimes i am tempted to ask God to have someone else take over, when what i should be doing, is praying for His strength and His direction. It takes me back to a time when there was a specific time every week when i was so very frustrated with everyone else just chilling and i was still having to work around the house even though i was so very tired! *But...* when i stopped long enough, at one point, to actually listen to the Holy Spirit speaking to my heart, i realized what i *needed* to do, was pray for God's strength, and be thankful that i was blessed enough to be able to do those tasks...i am telling you, it made a world of difference! So today, i am going to purpose to ask the Lord for the faith i need in His timing and His ways and to *stay diligent* in doing what is right because i love Him!!

"And let us not grow weary in well doing: for in due season we shall reap, if we faint not."
Galatians 6:9...

Faith

Firmly

Assured of God's

Infinite power and

Trusting

Him completely – no matter what

I have this written out on a notecard in my Bible *to remind me* of what i need to be doing and the thoughts and attitudes i need to have. God is my rock, the only stable part of life here on this earth. Thus, the word *"firmly."* As i think of the footage of "Hurricane/Super Storm Sandy" that i have seen, i think of those things that were what we considered solid, that are *no longer* solid. But God is not that way. His stability is always sure!! And that is where the *assurance* comes in! It also makes me realize that apart from trials in this life which cause us to rely on the Lord, we will never know that assurance personally. Going back to the thoughts of the storm, i cannot help but see God's power!! What a huge storm! 900 plus miles across! How can we deny His power?! But lest we get caught up in the devastation of this storm, we need to remember how much of God's grace and mercy can be seen, through all kinds of means, to help these people through the other side of this! Who knows the kindnesses and the contacts that will be made to show His love, as a result of all this, that would otherwise never happen? Then there is *Trusting*...reminds me that my perspective is not always God's perspective. To trust means there is a certain amount that i cannot prove or see, with my physical eyes. But i am *confident* that there is hope! And with God there is always hope! But only with Him! May He give us the faith, each one of us needs, to keep us focused on *His* ability, no matter how big or small the trial, we (or a friend) may be going through. As we take our cares to *Him* and truly let *Him* lead and care for us, we will not be disappointed in who He is!

Resting

Many years ago, a speaker came to our church and gave such a fantastic picture of resting in the Lord. I will never forget it. He talked about how when he was a kid, his dad used to have a hammock. He and his siblings used to crawl up in that hammock with their dad. They were completely dependent on him, laying like a blanket on top of him. They had no worries of tipping or falling, just completely at peace. Fully confident of being safe! And i think what a beautiful picture of how we need to rest in the Lord!! On the flip side, when i try to do things my own way, or start to panic, then the hammock starts to rock and getting flipped out and hurt becomes a given!...oh to rest in the Lord, like this man did in his dad, in his hammock!

God's Sufficiency

God does not put us into battle to see us defeated, but to show us how all sufficient HE is and what amazing things can come as a result of growing! When life is easy, we tend to be less thoughtful of how much God is doing. We also can tend to become a little more independent than we should be. But when the situation seems almost impossible, that is when we look to see what He will do! Those are the times that we grow in our faith!

Fully Dependent on God

I was thinking this morning, as i was holding Dante (one of the babies i watch) what a great analogy for how i should be with the Lord. Dante depends on me to hold him, to rock him, to feed him, to comfort him, and to spend time with him. He has no fear because he is fully dependent on me. That is how i should be with the Lord...secure in His arms, relying on Him for my every need, allowing Him to soothe me, spending time with Him, and trusting Him to remove any fears that i may have. What an amazing Heavenly Father i have!!

Self Sufficient

Thinking about all the things i am not, and all the things that God is! When i am weak, HE is my strength. When hope seems lost, there is always hope in HIM because HE is still in total control and HIS heart is loving and pure! When i have no clue of what to do, the Bible says to ask HIM for wisdom, and HE will give it abundantly (we just have to go to HIS word to know what HE has to say). None of us are self-sufficient, even when we think we are! It is God who has put the balance in the air we breathe and the water we drink. He gives us our immune systems and lets us live another day (and the list goes on). We are needy people, but God is enough!! We just need to learn to go to His Word and take Him at His word! Then, there is peace, rest, sufficient grace, and strength, to meet our every need! When we are weak, He is strong! And we learn that best by experience...

God Knows

So, the last time i was writing on my blog, i have to admit i was a bit discouraged. They had changed the way things were done...and i was also a bit frustrated because when God called me to start blogging, i had some very unrealistic expectations. But i am thinking this morning that when God calls me to do something, even though i may not have a clue of how things will actually come about, *He always knows exactly* how He will use it. And according to scripture, i am to obey and to trust...So as i sit here typing, i am doing my best to remember that it doesn't really matter how far reaching or how short reaching my words are because when the Lord gives His direction, He has a purpose for it. And in that case, i must remember that He does not waste my time! He has a purpose *whether i know it or not.* I don't know what He has called you to do. Whether it seems huge and overwhelming, or very insignificant, He will give you what you need to see it through. Please don't get discouraged because it is not what you thought it should be or as "important" as what someone else is doing. We must not get caught in the trap of comparison to others. God made each of us with a purpose in mind! So why not give our all to Him and let Him do the rest. The life He has planned for me is not like someone else's...and that is as it should be. I really will be most content and at peace, when i obey from a willing heart and leave the results to God!

Joy

Thinking this morning that joy is not a natural consequence of things, but a choice to rest in Jesus and to trust in Him. It does not pretend that everything is a fairytale. But joy is grateful and thankful because God is God over All!!!

Trusting God or Trusting Myself?

In my heart i know that God has a plan in all things. In my heart i know that His timing is perfect. In my heart i know that He wants what is best for me and that it is better than anything i could imagine! Because it will matter more than anything i could dream up, these are some of the things i know for sure! But what happens, is that too often, the things i don't know for sure tend to come in and choke out what i do know...which leads me to understand why it is so important to think about the things i am filling my mind with...God's Word? Man's words? God's thoughts or my thoughts? Doing things in my own strength or in His strength? My own way only ever leads to temporal enjoyment at best, but usually weariness. Weariness--because He is the best source of strength. Weariness because His ways are better, and He is the only source of true goodness in me. Ultimately, i must decide that i am going to trust God's heart of love for His children above all else!! It is the only place of true peace and contentment--and an absence of weariness!

God's Sometimes Unknown, But Perfect Timing

I am so glad for the Lord's timing and His ways, in every part of my day... in spite of what looked like a bad thing, i know He has His reasons. I walked out of Walmart with my check card and receipt in hand, only to get to the car and find i was missing the card! I looked and looked, and asked the workers, only to no avail. But! My friend had the same bank and had an 800 number on the back of her card to call in case of lost cards. That was the first "plus." So, i called and blocked the card (thankfully, i have a cell phone and could do that) that was the second "plus." The man blocked the card and told me that i could go to a local branch and get it replaced today...3rd "plus" was that i have a bank that is actually open on Saturday! And they were open for another hour! Also, another "plus" was that i realized it right away--can't imagine what could have gotten spent on it! So, after i took my friend home and had gotten out of the car at my next stop, what do i find, but my check card wedged between my trunk and my back window! I had an idea of how i wanted my day to go and when i wanted things to happen, but God obviously had a better plan! Not sure if i will ever know exactly what it was, but i can trust that He was and is always in control! (By the way, thanks Debra Salzman for keeping a level head and for helping me to do so as well.)

Faith

Keeping my faith in the Lord is a concept He has been bringing to mind a lot lately. That means no worrying, only trusting. It means that i must not try to solve, fix, or figure out things on my own. But i need to be still and watch HIM work. Years ago, i made an acrostic from the word faith. And that is what He specifically brought to mind this morning.

F irmly (steadfastly, un-moving)

A ssured (confident, no doubt) of God's

I nfinite (unending) power &

T rusting (relying on, resting in)

H im (not self!) completely (in every way) no matter what!!

God is God!! And i am so glad that nothing catches Him off guard, surprises Him, or worries Him. He knows exactly what lies ahead and how He is going to take care of things (even before they happen) so that we can know Him and His ways better. It has no "what if's" because He already knows. If i would just really grab a hold of that, then there would not be fears or worries in my life either! ...sounds like a goal worthy of my time!

What Should I Fight For?

I believe there are things in this life that the Lord wants us to "fight for"...but so many things that are preferences and/or opinions are the things we tend to make a fuss over or 'go to battle' for. Today i am pondering that we need to fight for...

- time with the Lord,
- opportunities to encourage each other,
- chances to serve one another,
- and opportunity to share the gospel with someone,

...those kind of things are the things we need to be spending our energies "fighting for."

You Can Not Box in God

As i scroll through people's' posts every day, on Facebook, i see a lot of cares, concerns, struggles, and frustrations. So i would like to share a quote by Priscilla Shirer--"Our God is predictable in His character, but unpredictable in His activity. You cannot box God in! When you put your lid on a box, it doesn't limit God: it limits your awareness of God. He's still moving and speaking, yet you can be unaware of His transcendence, His greatness, and His ability because it is outside of your little box." I am thinking back to 20 years ago, when the Lord brought us to Fayetteville. What a trying first year we had! We absolutely knew we were supposed to be here! He had made that very clear! But there was absolutely nothing that went like we had thought it would. I am so glad that i will never have to relive that year, but the lessons learned and the growing that God brought, i would not trade for anything! There have been several times in my life when it has been that way. This year the Lord is "refreshing my memory" of some of the things i learned back then, even to a point of giving me the same verse this year that He gave me then. But one thing that He keeps driving home to me is that just because i do not "see" Him working, does not mean that it is so. Take heart my friends and family. He is alive and working in ways that we cannot and in ways we cannot see with our human eye. Remember He is limitless and cannot be boxed in!!

With God All Things Are Possible

God never allows difficult circumstances in our lives to destroy us; rather, He desires to bring us to a point where we realize that apart from Christ, we can do nothing and that with Christ, we can do anything He wants us to do. So glad that in the easy and the tough times, my sufficiency and grace comes from the Lord!!

Remember the Things God Has Done

Thinking that to say i have faith in the Lord is easier than living out that faith all the time. In Old Testament times they used to set up monuments to remember what the Lord had done at that time. It is so important for me to remember the times when the Lord has answered prayers and done amazing things because it keeps me mindful that He can and will do them again! In fact, there are things that He does on a daily basis that fit that description; i just need to focus on seeing them.

"Where faith begins, anxiety ends; where anxiety begins, faith ends."
George Muller...

We cannot have both at the same time!

It may not always seem like it, but our God IS ALWAYS VICTORIOUS!!!

Yesterday, today, and for always!

True Trust Equals Rest

I am thinking this morning that when i say i trust in the Lord, in His will, and in His ways, it needs to show in how i approach this life. It is not truthful to say i trust Him, just to worry or try to figure out how i can put something together or how i can make something happen. True trust in the One who loves me more than anyone ever can, means that i cast my burden on Him and let Him carry it. It means that when i pick it back up, i give it back to Him (no matter how often that may be). It means that i honestly and truly rest in Him and that i trust His heart to be better than mine!! There will always be things that i don't understand or that i wonder about, but either i believe God is in total control, or i don't....Here's to a resting and trusting day for all of us who call Jesus our Savior!! He is always pure-hearted and loving!!

"Whoso Trusts in the Lord Happy Is He."

"Commit thy way unto the Lord, trust also in Him and He shall bring it to pass." ...though the whole passage in Psalm 37:1-7 is excellent food for thought!! Whether we are going through a hard thing or not, always keeping our trust and reliance on Almighty God is forever the right thing to do!!

God's Faithfulness

As i think about how we think we would like life to be--fun, problem free, and heaven on earth, i realize that it will never be that way this side of Heaven. But the other thing i know to be true, is that the Lord always keeps His word and takes care of His children. It may not be the timing we want (so as to avoid unpleasantness) or in the way we want. But we can be sure that He Will take care of us! It is in those times He proves to us that He is as faithful as He has promised!!

Trusting Is Not Dependent on My Understanding

Thinking this morning about the fact that sometimes it is difficult to fully trust God because i try to understand Him as i would another person, the truth is, that He is nothing like that! He loves perfectly! He is always faithful and always good! His motives and heart are always pure! Oh, to grasp that He is not like a fairy godmother, but so much better, better because He always does what is truly best for His children and what will bring true peace and contentment!! I want to see Him as He truly is!

Still Trusting

Pondering that to pray about what concerns me will only bring peace and comfort, when i truly trust the heart and ability of my Lord! Otherwise i am not really surrendering those burdens to Him. He is a better parent than any of us are, and He loves His children (I.e. Me) better than we love ours!!! He is also able to do what we can never do for ourselves or for others!...

Worrying or Trusting

It comes to my mind that worry comes in several different forms. I know this, because it is something i struggle with. It is not one of those sins that others may see, but it is sin nevertheless. So, i must see it as against God. I know we tend to excuse it, but it doesn't change the facts. Whether i worry or trust--both are a choice. I personally have a tendency to "ponder" how God is going to work something out. Then, i think, "well if He doesn't do it this way, maybe He will do it this way. Or maybe if i just say something to someone then they will 'get it,' or if i do such and such, then it will all be okay. Or if they read this book, or watch this instructional DVD, or do this Bible study then they will understand. Or when is God going to accomplish this? Are people going to have to struggle for a long time or will they learn quickly? Will they have to learn the hard way, or can they just wake up and just do what they should? Well, what if they resist? Will God have to do something drastic to get their attention?" Those are just some of my ponderings--and they can become consuming (in case you hadn't picked up on that). And all of a sudden, i realize that i am trying to figure things out on my own. How? When? How long? And all the while, i still have an Almighty God who has always been in control, is currently in control, and always will be in control! Wait a minute though...if someone else were reading my thoughts, would they really believe that i believe that?? God tells His children to trust and to rest in Him. And all those thoughts are definitely not trusting and resting. I am afraid that it has become a bit of a commonplace, sort of thing that we, even as Christians, can have a tendency to limit our trust in God to our own understanding. But He is never limited by my understanding or my imagination! His ways are beyond mine! And His abilities are pretty mind boggling!! If i choose to trust, it does not mean everything is all of a sudden going to come together by tomorrow, and the stress will be over. It does however mean that my focus will be on the Lord, and He will fill my heart and mind with His thoughts and perspective rather than my own. He will take the process that is necessary to accomplish His purpose (And generally, there is a process)! But i must say that the rest and peace that comes from trusting His ways, His time, and His loving heart, cannot be compared to anything else!! They are amazing -- no matter what is going on!! He never promised life would be easy, but He has promised to be my strength and guide and to give me grace sufficient for what i need. So i don't want to live thinking that somehow my "limited vision" limits my limitless God! Because it never does, it only makes me miserable in the process of life. He is a h-u-g-e G o d who is never limited by any box of any sort!! May we each live with that in the forefront of our minds!!

Obedience and Trust

God does not ask for me to figure out how He will do something but to walk in obedience, and to simply trust that He will accomplish it! Too often i want to figure out the details or how, or when, or in what order things will happen. But trust simply takes God at His word! Much easier said than done.

God is Always True to His Word

When i ask the Lord for direction in my day, i can trust that His Spirit will lead me. He will give those thoughts and attitudes He wants me to have. But i can also count on the fact that He will never counsel me in any directions or attitudes that would be contrary to His Word.

True Faith in God and Not Myself

Thinking that faith is required, if i am going to live my life first and foremost for the Lord...means sometimes He calls me to do things i may not quite understand or think i am capable of. But He IS faithful to equip His children to do what He wants us to. And if i say that i have faith in Him, as Savior and Lord, and don't have anything in my life to back it up, then it is probably not true faith. I don't ever want someone to think that is the case in my life! So here's to keeping my eyes and focus off of my own abilities and focusing on all that God is instead!

Trusting the Lord Even with the Weather

As i sat reading Facebook posts today, there was a lot of talk about the weather. No matter where you are - there are some who like it, and some who don't...and as plans get rearranged for many (myself included), i still am very much aware of Who it is that orchestrates the weather. And i am so glad that He sees everything clearly and none of it is purposeless. I know that no matter what, i can trust His will and His motives...after all it is not always about me. In fact, often it is not. But i can trust the Lord even in the weather. Here's to us all finding something to count our blessings about today! His mercies are new every morning!

Trusting Still

Today i am reminding myself that when i don't understand the process that goes with this life, at times, i must choose to trust the all loving heart of my Savior!! I must keep my focus on Him, and not the circumstances or people involved. I cannot change others or many of the circumstances, but i CAN choose to trust my loving Savior and Lord! He will carry, lead, and direct, as i seek Him and follow in obedience...

Trusting Means Letting Go

As i sit thinking this morning about trusting, i realize how easy it is to tell others to trust God, and yet not always so easy to put into practice the same thing...But numerous places where God talks about trusting Him, He also tells us how to exercise that. To cast our cares on Him means to throw away from myself and to let go! He also tells us not to lean on our own understanding...not to try and figure things out on our own, but to seek His direction and sometimes to simply be still...i have had several opportunities this week to encourage others to trust the Lord. Then, i find myself picking up things that i should not carry as well... But praise God for His Word which reminds me of those very good and right things that i have reminded others of. He loves me so much. He will not leave me to myself. The God of the Universe,

who is in control of all things

and loves me more than anyone else could ever love me!

When i set my thoughts there, then my focus ceases to be about me, the worries i carry, or anything that would draw my focus somewhere else. God's Word can have so much impact if i will obey what it says!!

Faith in God that Leads to Action

I am thinking this morning about how many times i have read, heard, sung, and even taught about David and Goliath....but this morning as i was reading in 1 Samuel, i realized what an inspiration it can be! David, described as a youth, comes into an army camp to check on his brothers for his dad and sees a man almost 10 feet tall. The giant is challenging and mocking the Israelites, and David wonders why they are not fighting him. God is on their side. It is pretty cut and dry to him. Courage and faith in God is so obvious to him! So, he goes to fight the giant with just a sling and some stones. He even assures Goliath that God will fight for them and that He will win. It is never about how strong David is but always about what God will do for His people. I know that some of the "battles' in my life are of my own making...but there are many that i do agonize over--when what i really need to do, (like David) is just have that faith in the amazing, Almighty God, who is my Heavenly Father! We sometimes talk about the foolishness of youth, but God commends the faith of a child...these are the things God has impressed on my heart and mind for today.

Trusting God Rather Than the Media

I have seen several things this past week about how Satan is proving he is at war with Christians. And all kinds of things are said in the media. I learned several years back, through up close experience, that the media is far from trustworthy!! I don't care how they may try to make it look. And it comes to mind, that rather than post articles or opinions we could accomplish so much more by praying!! God knows what did and did not happen. He knows how He plans to work good and show His glory and power in the process. So, it seems to me that prayer is a much better place for the rest of us to be focusing our attention...

God's Faithfulness

Thinking about the faithfulness of God...that He is always true to His word! Things may not happen like i think they will, or when i might like them to, but God will never go against His own character! He will also never "fit into any box" He is God! He is infinite! He is *beyond* beyond!!

Choosing to Rest and Trust in the Lord

"Trust in the LORD with all thine heart and lean not unto thy own understanding. In all thy ways acknowledge Him and He shall direct thy paths." Prov. 3:5-6. I am thinking this morning of where the world is at, at this point in time. Also, the many struggles that people have, on a more personal level come to mind. And they remind me of just how important this verse is. The Lord wants me to trust and rest in His care and to seek His direction. That doesn't mean, that all of a sudden, i will be living in a fairytale land, or that the hard stuff will suddenly become easy. But He does promise me that He will be with me and give me His strength! Oh, what peace and joy come when i choose to rest and trust in the Lord and do things His way, no matter what the circumstances may be! But it doesn't just happen, it is something i must decide to do.

Hope and Trust in the Lord

I am reminded this morning, that my hope and trust need to be in the Lord. That is not new news, but i find that it is easy to get distracted from it at times. Then, the perspective and attitudes of my life become more worldly and skewed. That is not what i want. I want to be what the Lord wants me to be, and to reflect Him most of all! Well, there i go... Goal set for my day.

I Can Always Trust the Lord

"We must never allow our questions to overshadow the fact that God has all the answers."--Priscilla Shirer ...I am thinking this morning that, as a parent, there have been times that i have had to say "no" or "wait" to my kids, because i knew something or understood something that they did not. I love them dearly, and it was because of that, that i had to say "no" or "wait." They probably thought they knew better, or at best, didn't understand my reasoning, but they had no choice in the matter. I was the parent, and they needed to trust my heart and my wisdom. I can always trust God's heart and His wisdom. He loves me perfectly, which means I have no need to fear, even if i don't understand or i question what He is doing. He is faithful, and His character remains the same!

Spiritual Growth / Health

Vitamins or Medicine?

I have been thinking lately that there is a tendency, for most of us, to approach reading God's Word like one of two things--vitamins or medicine. When one takes vitamins, it is to help prevent problems and to maintain health. It is usually done daily and systematically. I truly believe that is how God *wants* us to approach His Word–to read it on a daily basis, getting to know Him and *His* ways. That way when situations arise, we are more likely to know what He would want us to do and what attitude we should have, because we know Him better. But when one takes medicine, it is usually because the person is already sick. It is important to take medicine when we are sick...we need God's Word in the bad times as well. But, how sad, that at times, we wait to read His Word or even talk to Him until there is a major problem. Then, when He doesn't show us the answers we want, we get upset. But i would like to take it one step further and say that, like medicine, we should read God's Word, every 4 hours. How much faster things, especially our perspective, would improve if we were filling ourselves with His Word that consistently! Ever had a friend who only comes to you when in need of something? You don't necessarily turn them away, but you probably see the relationship for what it really means to them. So...vitamins or medicine? Hopefully, we will all *choose* to read God's Word as one would take vitamins–*on a daily basis*— getting to know Him and His ways so that when "life happens" (cause it will), we are well prepared, and trusting, and resting, in who we know our Savior and God to be!!

Change

Life changes, and with those changes come a lot of different emotions. But since there is nothing we can do about things changing, i realize that i must be sure to seek the Lord's direction about what my attitude is supposed to be. Some changes i love, and some– not so much. But the truth is that the Lord goes before me, and He has already checked things out ahead of time. He loves me (and all His children) more than i can ever fathom! And His Word says His plans are for us to have a future and a hope!! I used to use an analogy, years ago, about the Lord wanting His children to look like a diamond...a diamond has many facets to it (they pick up the shine). But for a jeweler to get that diamond to have many different facets, he must chip away at the rock, smooth those surfaces, and polish it. If i am to let the Lord shine through me, it will take life experiences, changes, growth, and all that 'stuff,' that brings with it all sorts of emotions...but i can rest in the Lord, and know, without a doubt, that it will be for good and not for evil...so, today, as life is changing for me, i am making it my goal to trust the Lord and to trust that He has new opportunities and people that He wants to bring into my life to make me a more faceted diamond for Him! Hoping someone who is reading this will be buoyed in spirit as well!

God or a Roaring Lion?

"Casting all your care upon Him; for He cares for you. Be sober, be vigilant; because your adversary the devil, as a roaring lion, walks about seeking whom he may devour: whom resist steadfast in the faith..."
1 Peter 5:7-9

As i read this, i am once again impressed by the fact that God has put things in a very specific order in scripture. I am to cast (throw) ALL my cares upon Him! And to follow that with a warning, definitely implies that if i don't, the devil is going to pick up on that! He does not want what is best for me, only what is best for himself. Now think about it... if a roaring lion were heading your way, would you try to pet it or get away from it?! This life we live is a spiritual battle! When i lose sight of that, it is bad because i get caught up in attitudes, and thoughts, and actions that i should not. Worrying about money, or friends, or family... fretting over paying bills, or what will or won't happen,... wanting things we don't have, wondering how we will accomplish the things we must do, becoming overwhelmed by whatever may be going on in our lives…all of those are "cares" that i (we) should be casting on Jesus! This life we live is a spiritual one–whether we lose sight of the fact or not. But which spiritual side am i on? Am i living a life of surrendering my cares to the Lord and living in faith in my ALMIGHTY GOD? Or am i trying to pet the lion without getting hurt, so to speak? I am pleasing one or the other.

Growth in the New Year

Well, it is a new year (2014), and the goal for me this year is to learn grace--also makes me think of wisdom, because it is getting to know the Lord better and reflecting that in my life. Knowledge is *not* where i should stop. God has created me to bring Him glory through the life that i live. The only way to do that is to get to know Him and to become like Him. If you are like me, you grew up in church, and sometimes it seems there is no other way to live but for the Lord. But when i stop and think about how much i have learned over the years, there shouldn't be anyone who doesn't see Christ in me. Unfortunately, that is not always how it is. But i am so thankful for God's Word because He gives me such clear direction! For an example, yesterday i was reading the verses in Ephesians 5, that talk about not worrying about anything, but rather praying for my needs, and also for the needs of others, and giving thanks. He doesn't just tell us what *not* to do, but what *to* do. I love that about Him! He knows i need more than just a clue. And when i look at this verse, i also realize that this is something that i have a problem with. Part of the problem is not just worrying-- it is understanding what worrying is. It is not just a lack of trust in the Lord; it is doubting Him! Ouch! That puts a much more pointed view of it being sin. But if i am to learn grace, then i must not focus on worrying (what i don't understand or what i don't see), i must focus on prayer-- for my attitude, my thoughts, my surrender…and sometimes similar things for others. I have thought about the fact that it is always right to pray for the Lord to give me His perspective! But i must not forget to do the last part of the verse...to give thanks! Thanks for what the Lord has already done, thanks for what He is doing right now, and thanks for what He will do in the future. Those things look so much more like Christ than worrying, or stressing, or becoming uptight or frustrated. I don't know what the Lord may want you to learn this year, but He does want you to learn. And it is always a good thing to become more and more like our Savior!

Learning?

Thinking over the fact that i have been a believer for over 40 years now. Because i put my faith in Jesus when i was very young, obviously not all of that time was spent growing in the Lord and in my relationship with Him. But as i got older, it became the desire of my heart to know Him better, and on a much more intimate level. So probably for the last 30 plus years, it has been a focus of mine. However, spending time with Him, has become a regular part of my day, and there have been times when i have not given it as much thought and energy as i should have. I say all that to say that in James, it says that we are to always want to learn. Do i always want to do that? Hmm...the older i get the more i do learn because of life experiences. But sometimes i realize that i have also gotten a little more stubborn. So, this morning i am reminded that my goal should always be to grow and to learn when it comes to my Lord! Years ago, i knew a dear old Christian man who had the philosophy that every morning he woke up, God had something for him to learn that day. That is how i want to be, not ever thinking that i know it all or living in a way that i would give that impression. Being willing to learn means i have to be teachable (which means i am *not* always right)...pondering this morning that that is a worthy thing to set my sites on!

In a Spiritual Battle

Thinking this morning about the fact that we are all in a spiritual battle on a daily basis, i need to not forget that. Otherwise, i will let my guard down. But i am so thankful that the Lord gives me all i need to wage this spiritual battle and win!! His Holy Spirit indwells me, and thus i am fully equipped! But if i think i am not in a spiritual battle, then 'the other side' is winning...so here's to putting our full confidence in the Lord and fighting the good fight of faith, in His strength!

Physical and Spiritual Growth Take Time

If you have ever been to my house, you know that our basement is a garden level basement--which means that it looks out at ground level. I love it because i have azalea bushes outside my kitchen and dining room windows! So, i especially like springtime! As i was looking across the room this morning, i could see one pink blossom. The rest of them were just buds. But the Holy Spirit gave me a picture at that moment, of a spiritual truth. He brought to mind that that blossom takes time to grow, to be watered, and to get just the right amount of sunshine to make it bloom. But if i were to go out and try to "force" the other buds to bloom by prying them open, it would definitely not have the same effect! I could peel back the green covering and they still would not just pop open! Or i could peel back the green and try to force the petals to open up, but it would basically just fall apart. Then, there would not be any blossom at all. It made me think of how i pray for things, and the Lord says it is going to be a process, and i am going to have to wait. Not usually the answer i want, but the truth is that growing, and being watered, and getting the right amount of sunshine, allegorically speaking, takes time. God will bring about the right conditions to make all those things happen in the right way and the right time. But only then will the blossoms bloom lovely and be reflective of our Artist, and Creator.

Whose Power Am I Looking At?

Thinking that though i have no power to change the happenings around me, the Lord still gives me the power to overcome their vice grip on my life and to rest in Him!

Growth

As i was looking out my kitchen window this morning at the many lovely roses on the vine, the Holy Spirit reminded me that they required both sunshine (heat) and rain to get to that point-- just like we need both the "heat and rain" in life, in order for us to be more beautiful and to reflect our Savior...not generally the process that i want, to become "beautiful", but the process that i need...

Refining

I am thinking about the things that are in the news that i wish were not...about how this country is no longer the religious and moral country it used to be. And those kind of thoughts can bring a certain fear and panic, if i allow them to. But as the Lord usually does, when i am willing to listen, He gives me more of His perspective than mine. I am so glad He does!! He reminds me that beauty and strength do not come about from life being easy. When a bodybuilder is working at building his strength, he has to bear through the pain to get there. Consistency and endurance are definitely involved! When a diamond is found, it does not look like what we think of as a diamond. The rough exterior must be chipped away and the different facets cut into the stone, before you see the sparkling rock we think of as a diamond. In the same way, precious metals must go through a refining fire to get rid of the imperfections. Only then do you see the real beauty that lies within...These things remind me that when life is too easy, there is not the beauty and strength that there could be. I look at our nation and think about how much freedom we have had over the years and how there are those who are trying to take it away, on numerous levels. But then the Lord brings to my attention the verse where it tells of how Joseph told his brothers that even though, they meant it for harm when they sold him, God meant it for good. Even though there was much that didn't seem good in that time in between, God had put him in a place and position to help keep his family alive! It is a fact the church has grown more when it has been under persecution. So, while i have never been a glutton for punishment, if i want my family in Christ to grow, then i need to realize that some things are necessary. Don't get me wrong; i am not saying that the things that are happening are wonderful. They are not! In fact-- people are trying to squelch the truth of God's Word. And i would never be in favor of that! But God is still God! And all that He does and allows has purpose! Good purpose for His children! No one has ever been able to completely do away with God's people or His Word! They have tried and never fully succeeded! And they won't! Friction, pain, and troubles are a necessary refining part of life. So though i would like to have things stay as easy as they have been in the past, i must realize that if i want to be more like Christ, then there must be those times of refining. I never want to lose sight of the fact that God is in full and total control!

Thinking today about the scripture that says, “With God all things are possible!” (Mark 10:27) and also that we can do all things through Christ who strengthens us!! (Phil. 4:13)

Time with the Lord Produces Christ Likeness

Proverbs 9:10--"The fear of the Lord is the beginning of wisdom: and the knowledge of the Holy One is understanding.".......Thinking this morning that when i know the Lord, when i really get to know who He is and His character and His heart, then i understand His ways. And i will trust Him! Not because of what i have seen Him do, but because of who i know Him to be! And i will come to be more like Him, loving what He loves and hating what He hates!

Focus on God's Strength

So thankful that my weakness = God's strength! Satan would like us to focus on our weakness rather than God's strength, because then we become stagnant and unproductive...here's to giving the Lord the victory instead!! Have a wonderful weekend my family and friends!

Spiritual Strength

As i was reading my Bible this morning, i came across a verse in Psalms where David is crying to the Lord, and He answered him. But God didn't take away his problem. He "strengthened his soul" instead. Often, we cry out to God, and because He doesn't remove the problem, we think He is not answering us (well for one thing, "no" is also an answer). But to give us inner strength to endure whatever the issue is, can be such a blessing, because then He gets the glory! No one will look at me/us and say, "Well, you can't possibly relate to what i am going through because you never have any problems." Ease is really not always what is best. No one grows without some sort of resistance that causes them to "build those muscles." I am so thankful for the inner strength God gives on a daily basis! Especially because much of spiritual warfare starts in the mind...my food for thought today...

The Learning Times

As i sit here thinking about the women's Bible study i have been doing on Exodus, and the children of Israel going through the wilderness, and how it compares to our own "wildernesses,"...my first instinct is not to want those times. But as i study, i realize that i really do not want to avoid those times, because that is when the Lord makes Himself known to me more clearly. Those are the times when i am more prone to look to Him and for Him. He knows me better than anyone else does! He knows what i need to learn and how i need to mature in my faith. He is an all loving and always faithful God! And the more i am in circumstances that may not be my choosing, the more i will have opportunity to see Him at work!! So very thankful for who He is!!

Spiritual Battle

In Joshua chapter 8, the soldiers of Israel are being sent to go to battle against Ai. At a certain point, Joshua tells them to wait outside the city, but to be ready...and it causes me to think about how, as believers, we are in a spiritual battle on a daily basis. To be armed for battle, i need to know God's Word--His truths. I also need to be obedient to His commands, trusting that His strength is greatest. Just because i may not "see" the enemy, by no means, means that it is not there. It is so important to be infused with God's Word and ways, being obedient to Him!

Words

Caring or Constructive Criticism?

I have been pondering today...there are, at times, those who bring their cares or burdens to my attention, and my first instinct is to relate. Have i been where they are? Do i have an opinion or advice i could share, or do i need to share my problems so they won't feel like theirs aren't so bad? But lately i have been wondering if that is really what my thought process needs to be...what if they just need to know that i care and will pray? What if they just need to know i love them and am sorry they are having a bad time? No critiques or constructive criticism, just love and grace--like i would want to have, if it were me. The Bible tells me to do unto others what i want to have done unto me...Hmmm, always room to improve in my walk with God and my relationships with others.

My Words

"The mouth of a righteous man is a well of life:" Proverbs 10:11
Makes me very conscious of the effect my words have...what kind of impression do i make with my words? Are they "life giving" so to speak, or are they 'life zapping'? Whatever i say, to whomever i say it, i want it to reflect Christ so that people are glad to have me around and not counting the moments til i am gone or stop talking...as a Christian i am indwelt by the Holy Spirit! My words need to always reflect that...

Do I Always Need to Speak My Mind?

I am pondering today the joy that comes from using the spiritual gifts God has given us and the *responsibility* that comes along with them too. God has given me the spiritual gift of encouragement/exhortation. I am also a bit of a "fixer." I want to help and try to fix when i can. The problem there, is that sometimes i get to acting as though others should listen to me, like the Holy Spirit somehow needs my help (which He obviously does not). I want to say things to "help people grow" and to make them wake up sometimes. And if the Lord is in it, it is usually done face to face or in a private message. When i started a Facebook page and started blogging, i did it with the intention of using my spiritual gift to encourage others. And i absolutely love when i can do that. But exhortation also means correcting or bringing something to someone's attention, at times. I cannot, however, assume that just because it comes to mind, it is something i need to post to a public place or even privately. Sometimes God just wants me to pray about it. Oh, that i would know the balance and seek God's direction rather than my own. It reminds me that when i love the Lord with all that i am, and others before myself, the little things in between will not be an issue. My desire is that the Lord makes me more like Him and less like me.

What Do My Words 'Taste' Like?

I read this morning about how a wise person's words are gracious, meaning they are beautiful, precious, kind, well favored, pleasant... they are the kind of words that show the character of Christ. I also think of how words come out of the mouth and think of the kind of flavor they have--sweet? sour? bitter? tasty? or something you can't wait to get rid of the taste? The Lord doesn't miss a single word that comes out of my mouth! So it is important that i realize that the listener cannot un-hear the words either....both should inspire me to be sure that i am letting the Lord control my thoughts and words....and as i sit here typing, i am thinking about our church's ladies' retreat this weekend, having a similar topic. Though i am unable to go, it inspires me to pray for them all, and to pray that the Lord will work. I love how the Lord puts those things together!!

The Effect of My Words

Thinking this morning (i know that is not exactly a surprise) that my words always have some sort of an effect. Is it one that is beautiful and pleasing to the Lord, showing that His Spirit lives within me? I am a talker and thus use my fair share of words each day. I am, however, accountable for the words that i type or speak...do they show Christ? And as i think of that, i remember, especially this week, the sacrifice He gave on my behalf! I owe Him my all because of His amazing love!!!! And my words are no exception!

The Flavor of Words

I was reading in my Bible yesterday morning about the words that come out of our mouths–

sweet ones,

learning ones,

pleasant ones,

healthful ones.

And it makes me think of the things i put into my mouth...sweet food, sour food, savory food, vitamins for health, water to quench my thirst, bitter things on occasion, and salty food. They all bring to mind a specific flavor. And whether i am taking it in or spitting it out, it leaves a certain taste on my tongue. And in that same way, are the words that i speak, except that they convey a certain "flavor" to the listener as well! Words have a huge impact! They either leave a pleasant or an unpleasant flavor to all who hear them. I want my words to leave a sweet, healthful, savory, thirst quenching taste, and NOT a bitter or sour aftertaste. The only way that happens is by yielding my heart and mind to the

Lord...and sometimes it means not sharing words. That self-control of keeping certain "flavors" to myself...i am so thankful that the Lord gave me this picture to help me be mindful of the words i type, and the words i speak! He knows what i need to help me best remember! Praying today that my words will be sweet to the taste! And that maybe by sharing this, others will be helped as well.

Guarding Our Words

Wisdom knows when to speak and when to keep quiet. Foolishness always speaks and always shares...praying that the Lord will guard my heart and my mouth. For out of the heart the mouth speaks...

Encourage Rather Than Discourage

Thinking this morning that i don't want to be one of those people who others see and try to avoid because of the words that come out of my mouth. Rather, i want the words that come out to bring encouragement and hope because that is what we have in the Lord! He does not always change our circumstances, but He is always with us and will see us to the other side of them. Wanting to encourage rather than discourage...goal for the day.

Words

Read this morning about the fact that with many words is more chance of sin...i like to talk. If you know me well, you know that. But it is so important that i use my words in a way that glorifies God and does not cause harm. The first step is to make sure my heart is right with the Lord. For out of the heart the mouth speaks (Luke 6:45). And it is easy to know that i should do this. But what happens if someone annoys me or i just know how i could fix their problem...maybe i should share that with someone? No. It is so much better to take the matter to the Lord in prayer! The Lord can work in my heart and the hearts of others in ways that we never can. My husband posted this morning the other verse that came to mind. It says to let the words of our mouth and the meditation of our heart be acceptable to the Lord (Psalm 19:14)...i want my words to glorify the Lord!

No Excusing Unkindness

As i was reading about the virtuous woman this morning (Proverbs 31), i came across the verse that says she opens her mouth with kindness...Seems pretty cut and dry...but as i ponder the implications of that, i realize that that means we are not to make excuses for unkind words...like, "I'm just having a bad day," or "They had it coming," or "Well, it's true." The Lord has given us so much, and we are so undeserving! Yet, He is still kind!! How can i possibly excuse unkindness on my part?! Admittedly, it does take some effort to be kind. First, i must surrender my thoughts and heart to the Lord--then the words will not be such a problem. And as i was rethinking these things, a goal came to mind. I need to make a point to be kind to others. How great would it be if we would make a point to speak something kind to at least 1 person a day!! I am thinking it would be so very encouraging to others, just like Christ would want us to be!

Mercy and Grace

Grace

Just GRACE!! Grace given to me by God the Father, the Son, and Holy Ghost! Amazing grace!! Grace or some form of that specific word is used 200 times in the Bible. Makes me think the Lord wants me to pay attention to it. So, i got out my Strong's Concordance (i am sure that dates me) and looked up all the ways that it is defined. This is what i found:

mercy, pity, goodness, bountiful kindness, favor, also praying these things for someone, useful, better, benefit, joy, liberality, pleasure, thank-worthy

WOW!! God gives me grace!! But it is not meant to stop there. His grace is to have such an influence on my heart, that it is reflected in my life towards others. God's grace –> to me –> to others –> to others...but i also realize that grace is *not* what i give to someone because they are always nice to me. Often it needs to be given in exactly the opposite situation. That can be hard at times. I must understand that n-o-t-h-i-n-g i do, earns me "grace!" Therefore, if i am going to reflect His grace to others, it is not about their actions or lack of actions. It is about *unconditiona*l kindness. I love that God is gracious to me! But it is not "earned," and until i truly grasp that, it will be very difficult to demonstrate graciousness to others. My goal is to glorify God in my life, so my goal must also be to show grace! Here's to us showing Christ to others through grace.

Mercy and Grace

I am thinking this morning that God's forgiveness, grace, and mercy, by no means, negate the fact that sin is sin! In fact, the reality is that only when i see sin for what it is (against God, and worthy of punishment and death), do i fully understand the enormity of the love of God! That He forgives me and shows mercy and grace!

So very grateful!

God's Grace and Patience

I am so glad the Lord gives us a fresh start with each new day! That His mercies are new every morning! I am also thankful that He never gives up on me, even when i feel like giving up. Those days do happen. Sometimes it doesn't feel like He is merciful because i am looking at things through my own perspective. But still He is merciful, even when i don't recognize it for what it is.

Understanding I Am Not Worthy of Mercy

Thinking this morning that unless we really understand what mercy is, we will not be thankful for the mercies of the Lord every morning. If i don't understand that it is goodness i do NOT deserve, then i may begin to think that God somehow owes it to me. In which case there is no thankfulness going on--just getting what i deserve... i want to be sure that i understand that the goodness i have in my life is because of the Lord, and not because of me. So, here's to a day of thanking the Lord for His mercies that He tells us are new every morning!

God's Mercy

Thinking about mercy this morning... i was reading in Psalm 136. It has 26 verses and all of them end with the phrase, "for His mercy endures forever." As i think of how amazing the Lord's mercy is, i also realize that by the definition of the word, i can do nothing to earn it. I definitely don't deserve it! But God gives it anyway, and it lasts for always! It never ends! It is not something He has to give! But i am sure thankful that He chooses to!!! In turn, i don't believe He gives it to me to have it stop there. I need to extend the same to others.

Showing Mercy

We are told to be merciful as God is merciful (Luke 6:36). What does that look like in everyday life? All goodness that i receive from God, is mercy! I am not deserving of any of it. I am thinking that i need to remember that when someone or something gets on my nerves and i am tempted to give back to them what they have dished out, does that show Christ? There are so many opportunities in a day to show mercy. Hoping we will all look for ways to do that.

God's mercy and forgiveness are on my mind this morning...He does not turn a blind eye to our sin; He deals with it. But He does not hold it over our heads. He forgives and is merciful. Praise the Lord!

God's Mercy

Thinking this morning about mercy...how grateful I am for God's mercy to me! And how I need to remember that it IS mercy. Not anything that I deserve! But then I also think of how much easier it is to receive mercy from God and others than it is to give it at times...but I am also to be merciful to others as the Lord is to me....Mercy..

Mercy and Forgiveness

Mercy and forgiveness are on my mind this morning. They are definitely something we want others to impart to us (at least I do)...but when it comes to giving it to others, it can be a little harder at times. Nevertheless, God calls me as His child to be like Christ! He showed the ultimate mercy and forgiveness on the cross!! He by no means deserved that suffering, but He gave Himself willingly for our sin!! I am so thankful for His mercy and forgiveness! And for the mercy and forgiveness that I receive from others Wanting to show Christ to others through mercy and forgiveness, today.

God's Grace and Mercy

Thinking about what God's grace and mercy mean...and what it does not mean. It does mean that God gives us better than we deserve and often not what we do deserve. But it does not mean that He is ok with my sin. My sin always has a consequence of some sort or other. It is an offense to God! Jesus paid the price that we all deserve on a cross...tortured and awful! I am so thankful for His forgiveness! But i do not want to lose sight of the rift between Him and me that is caused by my sin. So, my goal for today is to be sensitive and obedient to His Spirit!

Mercy and Grace Do Not Mean God Is Ignoring Sin

Thinking that the Lord is so very merciful and gracious, but He does not tolerate sin. Yes, He is patient. But sin is personal against Him!! So why would i think that He would be ok with sin in my life? He would rather illuminate the sin and have me turn from it by the power of His Spirit...and lest we think that we don't have that problem, because we may "categorize" sin, sin is sin. So, today's goal is to be sensitive to the Holy Spirit and His convicting me of any sin in my life and turning from it...I want to be a reflection of Him!!

Grace vs. Works

So i have been pondering in the last 24 hours or so, something that i see happening around us quite often. I see those who preach, what many would call "easy believism." Say a prayer, go your way, do your thing, and God will take you to Heaven one day. But then i see the other extreme where there are those so concerned about giving a false hope, that it then seems everyone's salvation is questioned almost to a point that it seems they are preaching salvation by works. *sigh* The Bible clearly states that we are saved by grace and not by works! To put my faith in Christ and the work He has done on my behalf does not mean i simply believe in His existence. It means i put my faith in Him and the work He did to cover the penalty of my sin! Amazing love! My sin is worthy of death, but He became my sacrifice! I am so thankful for that! The Christian life however does produce a difference. It doesn't all happen at once, just like a baby is not born full grown. We are His children, and He helps us to grow along the way. He compares us to sheep which should clearly remind us that our becoming more like Him is a process that takes our entire lives. We can be slow learners at times, but He is patient and the perfect parent!

"Marvelous grace of our loving Lord,
Grace that exceeds our sin and our guilt,
Yonder on Calvary's mount outpoured,
There where the blood of the Lamb was spilt.
Grace, grace, God's grace,
Grace that is greater than all our sin,
Grace, Grace, God's Grace,
Grace that is greater than all our sin."

A hymn that says it so well!

The Love of God

Easter–i.e. love in action!

The last couple of days the Lord has directed me to verses speaking about love. The one yesterday was in 1 Corinthians 13. It says that love does not seek its own (its own way or desires- the idea of putting others first rather than myself). Then, this morning, where i was reading it was talking about how a specific church was known for how abundant the love was that they had for each other. Then, of course John 15:12. So, i sit and ponder the fact that Christ demonstrated His perfect love for us when He went to the cross for our sins! My family and i have plans to sit down and watch "The Passion of Christ" movie this week. And whatever you may think of the movie, our goal is to watch it and really get a grasp of how much our Savior loves us!!! He didn't have to do that! And it is not like watching a fictional movie– because Christ really did go through the agony of being crucified and humiliated for us! Do i grasp that my sin took Him there?? No matter how "good" we may think we are, we are still sinful, and that makes us *worthy of everlasting punishment*! Only faith in God's gift of His Son, being sinless and yet dying for my sin, and rising from the dead the third day, victorious over death and sin, keeps me from that punishment!! When i put my faith in Him to be my Savior, His Holy Spirit

came to live within me. And now i have the power within me to love others as He has loved me! Selflessly, sacrificially, unconditionally, not because of who i am, but because of who God is! As Easter is around the corner, i am reflective of how great Christ's love for me is!! Easter is the foundation of the Christian faith! I want to love others in such a way that they see Christ not only loves, but He is love!!

"This is my commandment, that ye love one another, as I have loved you."
John 15:12.
(This was spoken by Jesus)

Weariness

Oh, how i long for Heaven at times. To be with my Savior and see things clearly through His eyes! To worry or fret, or to grow weary with the stresses of this life, no longer. But that is not what the Lord wants for me at this point in time because i am obviously still here (Don't get me wrong, i am not suicidal in any way, just the longer i live, the more i understand how glorious heaven will be!). So, how do i deal with the weariness and desires to change things that i have no power to change? Trust! Rest! Refuse to fear! Hope and strive to be pliable in the hands of my Lord. To be an encouragement to those who may have been where i have been. To be willing to be used of the Lord, for His purpose, rather than for my own personal ease. And all of those things take a conscious effort to accomplish! But all things are possible with God! Honestly, i have to tell you, that i would like everyone i know to get along and life just be sweet and easy–for a little while at least. But how do we ever know how dependable the Lord is, unless we see how He meets us in our need? I don't know how you are or what struggles you are going through. However, i do know that our God does not do anything without a purpose! And i know that He has a heart of love for His children! His love never causes fear because it is a perfect love! And He loves you and me more than we can ever imagine! Don't give up on Him! He is always faithful!! Take heart and be at peace because He will strengthen and sustain you, in whatever comes into your life!

Valentine's Day <3

Valentine's Day...is one of my favorite holidays, probably partially because it is also my anniversary. But as i think about it, i am reminded that God IS love! I have been married now (2014) for 28 years. Praise the Lord! He is the priority of our lives and our love, and that is why it works! And that is also why we work *at* it- because those vows were not only made to each other, but also before God.

But many things come to mind when i think of Valentine's Day. I love the decorations and all the fun little stuff that i can buy. My kids used to love it when we homeschooled because they could count on mom making it a party day. I love my husband and my kids, and my friends as well. So, love is a wonderful thing to me. God loves us and in turn, expects us to love others. But then it comes to mind that sometimes we put expectations on those we love, as to how they should approach Valentine's Day...and i think of those i know, who have been greatly disappointed over the years. And as i ponder that, i realize we are all, at times, in a place where we are looking to see what someone will do for us. But on the flip side, because God is love and He demonstrates that to us, why not be the person who looks to see what i can do for someone else? True love is selfless and wants what is best for other people, ahead of our own desires. So, here's to loving others like God loves us this Valentine's Day!

The Love of God

"The Lord is my Shepherd, I shall not want [lack]." Thinking this morning that He meets my every need! Physical, spiritual, and emotional! What an amazing God!! I deserve none of it, but He gives it freely and because He loves me more than i can fathom!! Thoughts to ponder.

When i think of the sacrifice of Christ, the words AMAZING LOVE come to mind!! But we have to grasp the sacrifice He made, to really understand how much He loves us!! Otherwise, we totally miss it...

God's Unconditional Love

Thinking about how God loves me unconditionally!! It isn't about a beauty contest or the things i can say i have done/accomplished (though if i love Him in return, i will want to please Him). I can come to Him anytime about anything, and He will listen and never turn me away!! What amazing love from the King of Kings and Lord of Lords!!

Marriage-a Picture of God's Love for Me

Thinking today about how marriage is a picture of Christ and the church...so as i think about the very best my marriage can be, i can grasp a fraction of the amazing love God has for me and the daily relationship He wants to have with me!

To Grasp God's Love

Impressed this morning with the fact that if i can just really get a grasp of the love of Jesus for me, then it will have a major effect on what i do, what i say, and the things i think/ponder! How i approach life in general!

God's Love, Greater Than Any Other

As i have been reading through my Bible, i have been in Song of Solomon lately. And as i am pretty much a romantic at heart, i definitely enjoy it. But as i was reading it this morning, it came to me, that as beautiful as earthly love is, it will never be perfect. Someone or something will disappoint, or someone will not be available when we wish they were. But God loves with a perfect love! There is never a time when He is unavailable, or pouting, or giving us a cold shoulder, so to speak. He loves us always, and His Word says that nothing can separate us from His love (Romans 8:39)! I am so very grateful that His love for me is everlasting and unconditional!! Amazing love that i will never quite comprehend!!! It brings a smile to my face and joy to my heart!

The Love of the Lord-- Valentine's Day

As i was reading in my Bible this morning, i came across verses that talked about blessing the Lord...and i thought about what a perfect day it is to bless the Lord!! He, after all, IS love! And whether it is a day you love or hate because of all the romance it involves, there is always the love of the Lord to celebrate! He loves you perfectly, unconditionally, and always!! There is absolutely nothing to be compared to His love for His children! So, here's to a day to celebrate His love for you and to show your love for Him in the way that you love others! Happy Valentine's Day!!

No Fear in the Love God Has for Us

"There is no fear in love, but perfect love casts out fear: because fear hath torment" 1 John 4:18. That is God's love for us as His children! As i think on this verse, i think about how i try to be a loving wife, mom, and friend. But the truth is that i do fail people. Sometimes i disappoint them or am selfish. I want to love perfectly, but i fall short. God never does!! And since He loves me perfectly, i do not need to fear! In other words, i don't need to worry, to stress, or to try to figure out things that aren't mine to figure out anyway. The choice is mine, as to how i use my energy. Resting and trusting in the One, who loves me perfectly, is a much better choice!!

Jesus Loves Me

Pondering the fact that i am a part of God's family! "Jesus loves me this I know for the Bible tells me so!" 😊 I don't have to understand it because i'm not sure i ever will! But how thankful and grateful i am!!!! Especially since i know i (and no one else for that matter) can ever earn it!! Praise the Lord, He loves me!!

God's Love for Me

Thinking that part of making it day to day, God's way, is by bringing my mind to meditate and ponder His truth. Today, it is on the fact that God loves me. Not because of what i have done, but because He chooses to. He loves me no matter what! When times are easy and pleasant, as well as when they are not so easy or pleasant. The ease of life or lack thereof is no indicator of His love for me. In fact, maybe the unpleasant days are an opportunity to see His love more clearly... His love for me does not change because of circumstances or because of my behavior! His love for me is ALWAYS perfect and good! It does not change! Praise His name!!

Perfect Love Casts Out Fear

Thinking this morning that scripture tells us that perfect love (obviously only God's love meets that qualification) casts out fear because fear torments (1 John 4:18). So, why is it that i worry, when i know that God is in full control of all things?? His desire for me, as His child, is to trust and rest in His eternal and unconditional love for me. In fact, He wants that for all His children!! Goal for today--to trust and rest in the One who loves me most!! And Who loves my family and friends, more than i can ever imagine!

God Is God and Still Loves Me!

Thinking about what a blessing it is to be able to have a personal relationship with the Lord! But also thinking about how important it is to remember that He is not a peer, but He is God! Lord of the universe! How amazing that He cares and loves me enough to take time for me!! He doesn't have to, by any means, but He chooses to!!

God's Love for Me

I haven't written anything in a while...but have been thinking quite a bit about the fact that God's love for me is perfect. That means there is nothing for me to be afraid of! And it is one thing to say it, but another to live accordingly and to truly trust His heart. That means understanding that, if i know how to show love to my children, then He knows how to show love to me even more (Matthew 7:11)! But if i get caught up in anxiety and worry, i will fail to see who He really is! Because i am too busy not trusting to take notice...worry is sin, and it accomplishes nothing! So here is to keeping my eyes open to the many ways that the Lord shows me He loves me! And to trust His heart completely!

Love for God & Others

The Greatest 2 Commandments

I was reading this morning about how, as God's children, we are to be righteous. There was also a verse right in the middle of the passage that talked about how Christ has defeated the devil (Hang in there, it will tie together). Then, it went on to talk about how we are to love one another. From there the Holy Spirit took my mind to other scripture that tells us that the greatest commandment is to love the Lord God with ALL that we are, and the second greatest commandment is to *love others as much as we love ourselves* (Matthew 22:37-39). And i am reminded once again why those are the greatest commandments. Because if i am loving the Lord with all that i am and honestly loving others as much as i love myself, then my actions, and attitudes, and thoughts, will fall in line in such a way that is pleasing to the Lord. Consequently, when i am living in that way, it brings about righteousness! And the devil's plans are thwarted! Christ defeated the devil through His death and resurrection! And there is never a contest between their power! They are not evenly matched! The devil only has as much leeway as God allows! I, on the other hand, am responsible for who i allow to have the victory in my life. Am i loving the Lord with all that i am and others as much as myself? Loving others as much as myself...wanting what is best for *them*, wanting comfort for *them*, wanting *them* to be shown kindness, and mercy, and understanding, wanting *them* to have good friendships, and happy families, food that *they* like to eat, for *them* to have blessings from the Lord, and His teachings. I don't know about you, but i don't always love others quite as much as i should. And to love the Lord with all that i am...means everything i do should be done with a mindset that i am demonstrating my love to Him! I am challenged today and encouraged. Challenged to love the Lord with all that i am, and to love others as much as i love myself. Encouraged because by loving them as i should, i will be righteous, and thwart the devil's attempts to bring me down at the same time! If i am not loving God, with all that i am, and loving others as myself, i am *not* being righteous. Love is not always a mushy, sweet, syrupy sort of thing, but it is always with a heart of wanting what is truly best for the other. May the Lord help us to love as He loves!!

Indulge Me

It is going to be David's and my 27th anniversary on Valentine's Day (2013)! So, i am rather fond of the day and the topic of love. But *please* don't tune me out because this is not just a post about romantic love.

Last night as i was reading a devotional book before bed, i came across a paragraph that i would really like to share. It is by Chuck Swindoll. And it says, "To love and be loved is the bedrock of our existence. But love must also flex and adapt. Rigid love is *not* true love. It is veiled manipulation, a conditional time bomb that explodes when frustrated. Genuine love willingly waits! It isn't pushy or demanding. While it has its limits, its boundaries are far-reaching. It neither clutches nor clings. Real love is not short-sighted, selfish or insensitive. *It detects needs and does what is best for the other person without being told.*"

It is evident to me that much of what we think of love, is actually selfishness. "Well, if you love me, you would________." But true love–perfect love–like God gives us and expects us to give to others is selfless love! Whether it is to a friend, or a family member, or a spouse, or a "significant other," we are to follow God's example. It can be tough at times. Our selfish nature gets in the way, a lot! But on the flip side, i wonder how much we would think of God, if He told us He loved us (like we tell others) and treated us the way we treat them...?! I want to love others like God loves me! After all, God says all our righteousness is as filthy rags–so none of us deserve His love!! But He gives it anyway!! I am challenged today, to be a better wife, mom, friend, relative...to love others the way that God loves me! And be ever grateful that His love for me is never conditional!! Happy Valentine's Day! God loves you and gave His Son on the cross to prove it!!

I Love and the Holy Spirit Fixes

There are times when i want to fix things or help others understand what i know to be true. But the truth of the matter is that the Holy Spirit is the best one to do that. Not that there are not times when i should say something...but not saying something is rarely the problem. 1 Corinthians says to follow after charity and that it always has an effect. So, the goal for today is not to "fix" anything or anyone, but to love those around me and let the Lord do the rest.

Love & Submission

So thankful that the Lord loves me

unconditionally,

perfectly,

and that His love is eternal!!

It makes submitting to Him a pleasure, rather than a drudgery!

I want to please Him because He wants what is truly best for me!!

Taking Time and Effort to Love the Lord More!

As i was reading my Bible this morning, i got thinking about how much i make time to connect with those i love throughout my day, to go see them, or talk, or just check up and see how they are doing, check their Facebook page...and it made me think about something someone said a few days ago about taking what/who you love the most and asking yourself if you love God that much. I need to love Him more! So today i am thinking that when i am excited about something i need to thank Him. When i see Him doing things, i need to express my gratitude. When i am sad or frustrated, i need to go to Him and His Word, to see what He has to say, and to get comfort from Him...after all, isn't that how i would be with someone i love dearly?? Thinking there is always space to grow closer to my Savior and Lord!!

Serving the Lord Because I Love Him

To be a servant to the Lord, is where my thoughts are this morning. And i realize that sometimes we bristle a little bit at being someone's servant. But the word servant comes from the word "serve"...and don't i want to please and to serve those i love? Of course, i do! I want to make them happy. So why wouldn't i want to please and to serve, without reservation, the One who loves me most? He is my Creator, and Savior, and Lord! His love draws me to Himself! So, here is to a day of serving the One who is the greatest part of my life!!

The 2 Greatest Commandments

Thinking this morning about what God calls the greatest commandments. The first is to love the Lord with all your heart, with all your soul, with all your mind, and with all your strength. The second is to love your neighbor as yourself. And i am reminded that when that happens, then the attitudes that i have, the actions that i do, and the thoughts i have, even the motives i have, will fall in line with God's character...sounds like a worthy goal for this day!

Love Produces Actions

The Lord has been speaking to me a lot about love this week. He has made me very much aware that the only reason i can truly love others, is because of the love Christ has for me!! But it is not enough just to say it. There must be actions put to those words...challenged today to be acting on those words "I love you"!...

Loved in Order to Love

Thinking this morning about how much God loves us!! And when we belong to Him, His Holy Spirit indwells us and fills us with His love. Not so that we can just keep it to ourselves, but so that we can share it with others. Then, they will see Christ because of the love we have for them.

The Impact of God's Commands

Thinking this morning about where i place value and importance. There have been times lately when i have struggled with whether anything i do has lasting value (Not fishing for anything, just being truthful). But then i am reminded of the 2 greatest commandments that God gives us...to love Him with ALL that i am and to love others as myself. I definitely do not love perfectly as i should. But i also realize that i minimize the impact that that has for Christ. So i am thinking this morning that maybe i need to simply obey those commands, that the Lord deems most important, trusting Him to put the rest of it in place.

Loving the Lord

Thinking about being obedient to the Lord and pliable in His hands...like a child should be with their parents (And i realize that there are those times when i struggle more with this than others). But it also comes to mind that the more i love someone the more i want to please them! And as i see how much they love me, it also makes me want to please them! Consequently, it is so very important that I spend time with the Lord and nourish and strengthen that relationship!

Surrender

To Be Still or Not to Be...

As i reflect on the fact that the Lord has given me the goal of being still this year (2013), i realize just how still i am not, at times. How much i desire to be fully yielded to the Holy Spirit as He leads, and convicts, and directs, and redirects in my life!! And the Lord reminds me that i have to let go of things, trying to control things. Things like hurt feelings, anger, frustration, family members, friends, fear, disappointments...and the list can go on. If i am honest, these are the things i hold onto. The problem is that if i hold onto them, it creates distance between me and my Heavenly Father. And that is a distance i DO NOT want to be there!

He is:

My Father, Savior, Guide, Lord, Shepherd, Best Friend,
Perfect Peace, Strength, Refuge

He is everything i need!

Why in the world would i want to distance myself from Him?! Why do i get so caught up in how i think things should work, or go, or be done?? It is not as though i can really do what only God can do! My Heavenly Father is the perfect Father!! *HE will* truly work all things out for our good (yes, OUR good) and for His glory!! And either He is always true to His promises, or He isn't. It can't be both. So i am going to try to step aside, stop trying to do things my way, be still, and pray. I want to let Christ do what He wants in me. And focus my eyes to look forward to the blessing of seeing His hand at work!

Releasing the Burden...

It comes to mind that i have been trying so hard lately, to be there for some people, who are very dear to me. They are having a hard time, and i want to give encouragement and guidance. And that is right and good. I would not, not be there for them. But it is also very evident that *i* cannot change their actions, behaviors, or responses…and it takes me back to another time, many years ago, when the Lord put someone back in my life, whom i had lost touch with for quite some time. Like now, the Lord would make it very clear what i needed to share with her, in her time of need. But i could not make her act on it. It is hard for me to accept the fact that though the advice and encouragement may be Biblical and good for their use, and even what i know the Lord wants them to hear, it is not my job to change them. I am accountable to come alongside in love and care and to share what God says in His Word. But they must take responsibility and be pliable in the hands of God! But then, it is as though a light bulb comes on in my head, and the Holy Spirit makes it clear that if i could just give people an "anecdote," and things be all better (which is what i would like sometimes), then *they would never understand that* they need to spend time getting into God's Word and getting to know Him. *And how very sad would that be!* Because i am not their Saviour or their Lord, and i will not constantly be there by their side. God, however, will always be by their side! Then, ever so sweetly, the Holy Spirit reminds me that His ways are not my ways because His ways are so much better!! I absolutely must rest there! Thank You Lord for enlightening my mind!

Comfort Zones

As i sit here thinking this morning, i realize that we all have certain comfort zones. I believe that the Lord often gives us those, where we are obedient and have our spiritual gifts. And that is a blessing.

But i also know that there are times when He calls me to do things that i am not as comfortable with. For whatever reason…it may be i have not done that sort of thing in a while (kind of what applies to me at this point in time), or it may be something i have never done before. But if the Lord wants me to do something, it is not about whether i am comfortable with it or not, it is about being obedient and trusting Him to put it together as He sees fit (including the outcome). Oh...that letting go of my own self-confidence and allowing Him to use me as His tool, that is the hard part! To be willing to go where maybe i am uncomfortable and watch what He can do, rather than what i can do! Aren't i supposed to be more concerned about others seeing the Lord and not myself?? Then, through my weakness He is strong, and others will see Him! May each of us have the courage to let go of our own insecurities and let the Lord's character be seen in us! To let go of our comforts and be obedient anyway. And to Him will be the glory!!

King?

"In those days there was no king in Israel, but every man did that which was right in his own eyes." Judges 17:6...We don't have kings here in the US, but the Lord needs to be king of my heart and life. That is not like our government here–it is not a democracy. A king has absolute rule no matter what! Do i give Him that? I am afraid that at times, i do a lot of things just off the top of my head, without hardly a thought. But the truth is that i do not belong to myself. I belong to the Lord! If i stop honoring Him as King, there will be great loss, on many levels! So, my challenge for myself today is to make sure that i am honoring the Lord as King in my life and consulting Him about the choices i make. Trusting the Holy Spirit to help me keep this focus. And maybe encourage some of you reading this, in the same direction.

Who is Leading?

This morning, as i read about the first king of Israel, Saul, i was realizing that he did things his own way rather than God's way. For whatever reason, it began to happen more often, and seemingly without much difficulty. I do believe we are all like that...the more frequently we do something, the more like second nature it becomes–very little thought or guilt. It is so important that as i live my life day to day, i allow the Holy Spirit to direct me, and i listen to His warnings as well. The older i get, honestly, the less likely i am to think i should change my ways. After all, i know what i am doing. i have been around. The problem is, that this side of Heaven, i will always have things that need the Lord's refining. So as i start my day, i am challenged to be sensitive to the Holy Spirit and His leading or halting in my life...because no matter how old i get, i will always need His leading and direction in my life!! I am so very thankful He gives it!

Burdens

Sometimes my heart *absolutely breaks* when i want, *so badly*, for someone i love, to be right with God. It tears me apart because i know how much better life in harmony with Him can be, than what the world has to offer. I *long* for them to know the peace and contentment that comes when we realize we are *not* our own and we owe our *all*, including our obedience, to Him. We need to not only admit our guilt, but turn in repentance from it, and to Him. He *will* welcome us with open arms! It is not something that makes sense to the world, but oh the joy that comes, when we truly surrender to Him!! After all, His Word says, His yoke is easy and His burden is light (Matthew 11:29-30). Even when there are consequences to my sin, He is merciful and gracious! Always! Because that is who He is! But i am wrong to think that my sin is not against Him. It causes a definite rift between us! He wants us to run to Him for forgiveness, wisdom, and refuge! He loves His children! He wants so much for us to know Him–intimately, as our *Heavenly* Father! And for our relationship with Him to be what it needs to be. There is nothing like it! His ways are not my own, but He loves me, and those i love, more than any of us can possibly fathom! On my part, i am responsible to trust the Lord to do the work that needs to be done in the life/ lives of those i love. I too, must surrender not only myself, but my cares to the Lord! So, i must also obey to be right with my Lord!

Surrender Day In & Day Out

I was reflecting on what i read this morning--about God's chosen people turning back to Him, after doing their own thing for so long. I was struck with the thought of surrender...and though i am not at a place where i have turned my back on God, i do realize that surrender is something that i must always be aware of. Sometimes it is easier than we think, to be drawn away from that, with the things of day to day life. I need to surrender all of myself, and all that i have to the Lord. Sometimes that comes in a little different form than we may think, but it is so important to be surrendered to the One who has saved my soul!! I owe Him everything! Though He owes me nothing, everything He is and does, benefits me in some way or another! True surrender to Him really is a joyous thing!

To be worried, or stressed, or frustrated, is a sure sign that i am not surrendering everything to the Lord....so when i see those things creeping up, it is time to give it all back into the Lord's hands!

Christ Our Perfect Example

Thinking about the fact that when Jesus knew His crucifixion was coming, He was still surrendered and obedient to the Father! He didn't have to be! He could have chosen a different way or decided it wasn't worth it. But instead He was our perfect example. He showed us His love even in His surrender!

Daily Surrender

Thinking that being surrendered to the Lord takes a consistent seeking of His will in every big and little part of my day. That requires that i make a mental effort at the beginning of each day to seek Him. It does not necessarily come naturally. But it will definitely be worth the effort in the end!

Thinking how important it is to be surrendered to the Lord! To be a servant to others, is also about surrendering myself to Him! My goal should always be in those directions! It is called being like Christ!

Surrendering My Cares to the Lord

How am i to deal with my cares and stresses? Some would say, talk them out. Others would be an example of worry and frustration. Some would get mad, because then, it "hurts less." But the thing that comes to mind, is to cast all my cares upon the Lord, because He cares for me (1 Peter 5:7). Does that mean i will always understand His ways or His reasons? Most likely not. But it does mean that i choose to give Him the cares and let Him do what He knows is best. He may reveal that to me, or He may not. Either way, i can rest in His loving care! After all, He loves me beyond my human comprehension!!

God's Ways or Mine?

Thinking about evil kings this morning...and that at the root of evil, is pride. These were men who loved and abused their power. Because of that, they suffered the consequences. As a Christian, my desires and goals should be to have God's will and desires, first and foremost! Not my own. If there is a disagreement between those 2, then i need to relinquish my will for His. When i put my trust in Jesus Christ, i surrendered myself to Him! Every part of me belongs to Him. So, when my pride gets in the way, i need to see it as a red flag--warning me to watch out. That can be hard, when this world we live in, would have it to be all about self. I am so very grateful that Christ came to minister (not to be ministered to)! He didn't have to! He had every right to demand the worship of a king! But He served instead. He is the perfect example of humility!!

Choosing to Let Go and Let God

Pondering...are you surprised? This morning i am thinking about the fact that left to myself, it is very easy to be stressed and full of worry. Trusting and resting in the Lord, is a choice i have to make on a regular basis. It makes me think of a young child who is tired, but refuses to give in and go to sleep. As adults we look at them and think, if only you understood how much better it would be if you would just go to sleep. Even that young child has to give up their play time and get some rest. We, as their parents, know it would be so beneficial--to all! And it makes me think of me with my Heavenly Father. He offers peace and rest! He knows how much better off i will be when i let go of the worries and trust Him! But i have to make that choice. So, do i want to be like that well rested little one or like the one who refuses to rest and gets grumpier and more ornery by the minute? It is my choice...

Letting Go Is Sometimes Necessary

As i was reading in Joshua this morning about how the Lord told His people to go in and burn Jericho to the ground, i was pondering the thought of total destruction before His people took over the land...and as i was thinking, i realized that often there are things in my life/our lives that keep us from being all that we can be for the Lord. Sometimes He knows that those things need to be completely removed before He can create the masterpiece He wants to make in me. I don't always fully appreciate that. But as a parent, i realize too that there were times when i had to remove things from my kids' lives, for their own good. How wonderful that my Heavenly Father sees my life so much more clearly than i have ever seen my kids' lives! So i am challenged today to be sensitive to the leading of the Holy Spirit. I need to let go of whatever it is that is standing in the way of being all that He wants me to be. To let Him have total control, and not complain, or hold onto what He says to release....

Casting Our Anxieties on Him

Wondering today, what a graph of my worries and anxieties, versus my prayer and surrender, would look like...the Lord tells us to cast our anxieties on Him! He tells us to trust and rest in Him! He tells us He will carry us and our burdens! He tells us He will give us His strength! So much He offers to do for His children!! Now if i would only live moment by moment like i take Him at His word!!

Beauty

Beauty

As i got ready for my day this morning and was looking in the mirror, my thoughts went to the way the world views beauty versus the way God views beauty. I think, women especially, struggle with the idea of having to have a specific kind of outward appearance. I must be toned and firm, hair just so, make-up just right, and of course the right clothes that fit you in a flattering way. And none of these are necessarily a bad thing, unless they become my focus. It is hard, i must admit, to stop and wonder what God sees when He looks at me each morning. The Bible says that He looks at the heart. As i got out my Bible and started to look up what God had to say about women, i found that nowhere does He emphasize her looks, but always her character...things like being kind and hardworking, wise and strong, thrifty, trustworthy, good to her husband (if married), sacrificial for the sake of others, helping the needy, praised by her family, modest, not drawing attention to herself, godly, Spirit-controlled, loving, discreet, pure, good to others (Proverbs 31, 1 Timothy 2:9-10, Titus 2:3-5). As i was looking these verses up and meditating on these things, my mind went back to many years ago, when i met a very beautiful lady. She was short and rather round, but always smiling, and she just seemed to exude the Lord! She is still a gorgeous woman in my mind, though she has been with the Lord for some years now! By the world's view she was not that way at all, but they miss so much by only looking at the reflection one sees in the mirror. That reflection is going to fade over years. But as a Christian woman, my godly character should grow more and more beautiful with time. That is my goal...besides when the beauty of Jesus is seen in me, then the outward appearance will fade in comparison.

Where Does True Beauty Lie?

I don't have an amazing figure or a flat stomach. I'm far from being considered a model but, i'm me. I eat food. I have curves. I have more fat than i should. I have scars because i have a history. Some people love me, some like me, some might hate me, but i hope not. I have done good. I have done bad. I love my pj's, and i go without makeup and sometimes don't do my hair. I'm random and crazy. I don't pretend to be someone i'm not. I am who i am. And if i love you, i do it with my whole heart!! And i hope that when i make mistakes (because i will), the Lord will show and redirect me, and others will be patient because He is not finished with me yet. Ladies, let's be thankful for who God made us to be because His plan is perfect!

Let the Beauty of Jesus be Seen in Me

Thinking this morning that this culture tends to breed discontentment...specifically in the issue of beauty.

One always needs to be prettier, or look younger, or skinnier, or be better dressed, or....and the list goes on. As i sat down this morning with my Bible, God says that He makes all things beautiful in His time. That means all! Beauty is in the eye of the beholder, yes. But whose beholding am i trying to impress? Peoples'? Or my Lord's? I can do all the things that are supposed to "make" me "beautiful", but if i don't have Christ-like character, the outer beauty will make little difference. Oh, to have the mindset that my most important beauty secret would be to be like Christ!

Beautiful Spirit? Beautiful Face?

A kind spirit generally has a much more lasting impression than a beautiful face. It is also what the Lord is most concerned about. Hmmm...makes me realize where my priorities should be.

Inner Beauty Vs. Outward Beauty

Thinking that the idea of outward beauty is dependent on who is doing the judging...everyone has their personal preference and opinion. But God's Word never emphasizes the outward beauty of a woman. He however often talks about the character of a woman. If i have outward beauty that draws people's' attention and yet lack Christ like character, the outward beauty is of little value. It is so easy to get caught up in the world's standard of "beauty," but what matters is the heart and what God sees there. THAT is what is truly important. And whatever goodness is found there, is His to receive glory for! ....

Beautiful in God's Eyes

Pondering this morning being beautiful in God's eyes...which i am reminded is the One i need to be most concerned about! And i realize that true beauty comes in godly character.... "But the fruit of the Spirit is love, joy, peace, long suffering (patience), gentleness, goodness, faith, meekness (strength under control), temperance (self-control): against such there is no law." Galatians 5:22,23 Reflecting Christ is always beautiful!! So, here's to a day of focusing on being pliable in God's hands and spending so much time with Him that i look like Him!

The Beauty of Jesus Seen in Me

Pondering this morning that when Solomon built the temple it was a work of amazing beauty!! Because of Christ's work on the cross and the indwelling of the Holy Spirit (because I have put my faith and trust in Him), God says i am His temple...and though my physical beauty may not catch everyone's eye, it is so important that the beauty of Jesus be seen in me!!

There is a song on my mind this morning.... The lyrics say, "Let the beauty of Jesus be seen in me, All His wonderful passion and purity, O Thou Savior divine, All my nature refine, Till the beauty of Jesus be seen in me."

Focus

Choices

As i sit thinking about what to write, i think about all the choices i/we have to make, about all kinds of things. Some of them seem quite simple and some not so much. How often do i consult my Lord about the choices i make? The worries that go through my mind...do i consult Him or just keep feeding my worries? Trying to decide what to do about a certain situation...do i ask His guidance or just fret about it? When i am frustrated, do i take it to Him or just let it build and build? God is always with me! Why is it that even though i know He will give wisdom and peace to those who ask it of Him, i forget/fail to do so? Oh, how patient He is! *But* how much i long to be more and more like Him, and in tune with Him, with each passing day! To lift my voice to Him in everything! The more i spend time talking to someone and listening to them, the closer the relationship becomes...hmm, i think there may be something to that...

Thoughts Fixed on the Lord

Thinking this morning that focusing on and worshipping the Lord, are always a safe place to be. Actually, they are the best place to be! He is to be first in my life! When He is, everything else will fall into place. I don't meant that everything around me will be perfect. But when He is first, then it is HIS perspective that i will have. That is what will help me appreciate all the blessings and endure the trials. Who God is...what a magnificent place for my thoughts to be!

Focus

Thinking that where my focus is, really does determine everything. It decides the truth that i am willing to listen to (God's truth or people's' opinions). My emotional state of being (encouraged because the God over all, is in control of it all!) is most certainly affected. And my expectations are determined as well (He works all things for the good of those that love Him, i.e. His good...which is always best!)! Today i am focusing on looking to the face of Jesus!

Hazards of Multitasking

Thinking today, that we women tend to pride ourselves in multi-tasking abilities. And as a mom, i know that at times, it is necessary. But as i look at my own life, i see how it can have a bit of a negative effect, as well. If i am not careful, it can become a habit to do too many things at a time; then, nothing gets done quite as well as it should. After all, i am to do all that i do as to the Lord and not unto men (Colossians 3:23). I am to give the best in all that i do because it is for the Lord. The other thought that comes to mind, is that when i am trying to do too many things at once, no one gets my undivided attention. What if God did that with me?! Really think about it! It would be horrible!! When someone talks to me, i need to stop and listen. Just like when i sit down to read my Bible and pray, i need to be focused and listening to the Lord, rather than letting myself get sidetracked. I just can't help but think that trying to multitask all the time leads to some of these problems...pondering

Focusing on God's Goodness and Power

Thinking this morning that i love how God puts together what i am reading in my quiet time, with what i need most for my day! I woke up today, being a little frustrated with something i knew i needed to just surrender to the Lord. It got me thinking i would be spending most of my day giving it back to Him. But as i picked up my Bible and started reading where i am at in the Psalms, He brought me to verses about exalting Him, and praising Him, and blessing His name. He had me reading verses about how His power is beyond my comprehension! Now

THAT is where my focus needs to be! Not only does it direct my thoughts off of frustrations (and what i can or cannot do), but it turns my eyes and thoughts to Him and to His power!! That is my goal for the day--that no matter what comes my way, i will continue to look to the Lord, and His goodness, and His amazing power!! He does so much on our behalf, as His children!! Praising is so much better than worrying or complaining! So... that is my goal for the day!

Where Are My Energies Focused?

Evaluating this morning as to whether i am giving more of my time and energies to the selfish things of this world, or to the things of Christ. I know what my heart's desire is, but need to be mindful that it takes an effort and a choice to make the Lord my first and foremost priority in a world that tries to distract us in so many ways!

My Heart Is Fixed

In Psalm 108 it says, "O God, my heart is fixed, I will sing and give praise, even with my glory." That word fixed comes from a Hebrew word meaning to be erect and established. As i thought about that, it brought to mind that if i am standing erect, i am unashamed and upright (both physically and spiritually, by His grace). Also, it means that if my heart is fixed on the Lord, then i am unworried, and consequently at peace because i am trusting the One who is holding me up and can never fail!! So why wouldn't i want to sing and give Him praise!! He is definitely worthy of the glory!

God's Character

It's been on my mind the last couple of days, that it is always a good thing to focus on the Lord and His character! Never is it a wrong thing to do! He is Creator God. He is Almighty! He is Counselor, Teacher, and Guide! He is love! He is mercy and grace! He is the most amazing artist ever!! He is faithful and true! Never do i need to worry when i am in His care! The list is endless!

Focus on God's Character Alone

So often as i read scripture, i do so with a perspective of looking for ways to be more like Christ (And that is necessary and important). But this morning as i was reading, the Holy Spirit impressed on me that i needed to just focus on God and His faithfulness! Sometimes i can become so focused on what i should or should not be doing, that i lose sight of The One that i am wanting to please. I am so very thankful for His unfailing love and faithfulness!! ♡Here's to a day of focusing on who He is!

God's Amazing Creation

I just watched a slideshow that reminded me how much of God we see around us on a daily basis! Yet at times, we are given to worry and complaining. What we should be doing is focusing on all the many amazing things God has created and done!! A MUCH better thing to spend my time thinking on! His creation is just a small demonstration of His enormous love for His children!!

The Blesser or the Blessing?

I am thinking this morning about how when God blesses me, i need to not be so distracted by the blessing that i forget about the Blesser! He is still the One who deserves to have my focus! Always!

Keeping My Focus on the Lord

Thinking today about the many many distractions (both good and bad) that come my way on a consistent basis. But i want my priority and focus to always be on the Lord. So how do i do this? It must be a daily commitment and a conscious effort to ask Him for HIS leading in my life. Everything that is good is not necessarily my responsibility. I want to be used where HE wants me to be ministering. I also read, from 2 different sources this morning, things that reminded me of a wonderful way to keep my focus on the Lord--through singing songs of praise to Him. We don't have to have a trained voice. He simply wants us to make a joyful noise to Him!

No Complacency

Thinking this morning that complacency is one of the devil's greatest tools against Christians. It is so important that i am seeking God's focus and direction on a daily basis and InTeNtIoNaLlY following it! Obedience is a must!!

More Is Not Necessarily Better

Thinking this morning that more is not always better. Contrary to what our tv commercials try to tell us, sometimes more is just more. In fact, sometimes it can actually be a problem. Because sometimes more can distract me from what it is the Lord really wants me to focus on. Sometimes the Lord wants me to learn contentment with less. Many reasons why more may not be better...things i am pondering this morning...

Distractions Anyone?

There are so many distractions that this world offers us. I am thinking about the fact that they are not necessarily bad in and of themselves, but when they become what we look for on a consistent basis, there is very little contentment or satisfaction. As i sit thinking this morning, i realized that when "distraction" is what my life is about, the balance is very off kilter. God did *not* plan for my life to be just random stuff, filling my days. He is not random. Everything He does has purpose (even when we don't see it). There are obligations i have chosen in my life, but when i start looking for distractions, those things cease to be accomplished like the Lord would have them to be. As i thought about these things, the commandments that God called the greatest came to mind. To love the Lord your God with all that you are! And to love your neighbor as yourself! In other words, i need to be sure God and people are my first priority, and in that order. When they are, then i will be both obedient and content. I will be honest with you...lately, i have lacked direction. But as i ponder it, i realize that i have been looking for those distractions, rather than for what it is the Lord wants me to do with my days. I do belong to Him! And by experience, i know that i am happiest when i am walking according to His will and surrendering my days to Him. There are specific things i *know* He wants me to do, and those should be my first concern. When i need a break, He will provide it. I just need to be careful not to throw the scale off balance with "distractions." So here is to a better focus and direction!

Praise

Praise

I don't know about you, but i'm not always consistent at doing this. There are times i am tempted to complain, rather than to give Him praise. There are times i am tempted to fuss, rather than to let my mind be filled with His praise. There are times i am tempted to worry, rather than to remember to praise the Almighty God, who is still in control.

And there are times i am tempted to stress and try to figure things out on my own, rather than to rest and praise the Lord, for the peace He gives, in spite of whatever is going on.

To praise Him continually means i have to let go of my cares and rest in His care! I don't know if you have ever been in a place where life just seems stressful for whatever reason, and you are on edge all the time. Then, you realize that you need to rest in the Lord and let Him take control. The peace that comes from letting go of the cares and letting Him have them, is *beyond compare* to anything else!

The other thought that comes to mind is that, as parents, we do certain things for the wellbeing of our children. Sometimes they don't understand them or like them at all. But because it is for their best interest, we stick to our guns! Why would i not want my Heavenly Father, who sees all and knows best, to look out for my wellbeing? Just because i may not understand it or even like it? Well, if i truly believe He is who He claims to be, then there is no issue. I can praise Him in the hard times, and the good times, and all the in between times! He is worthy of my praise *on every level!* I should consider it a privilege to give it to Him!!

"I will bless the LORD at all times: His praise shall continually be in my mouth."

Psalm 34:1

Past and Present

When we have a hard time thinking of anything good, we can always rejoice in the Lord. When we realize how amazing His character is, the things around us seem to pale in comparison. So much in this world we don't have control of, but God's character is always dependable, constant, and true! *He never fails!*

So…if you have known me for a long time, you may realize what this day is, but if not, you are clueless. I say that because i am in awe (often) of how the Lord puts things together, so that we will remember or learn something a little better. Eight years ago today, my husband was in a horrible accident (there were those who told me, after the fact, that they did not think he would survive!) The spiritual goal that God gave me that year was patience…and patience we learned! None of his injuries were the kind that had a specific time frame of healing. We were simply told it would take time, and we would just have to wait and see how things went. Well, i am here to tell you that the Lord turned my focus to His character! Nothing was in our power to control, but it was all in His power to control! And since He focused me on His character there was peace and hope! The patience was a process. Paralleled to now–the spiritual goal He gave me this year is to "be still" (definitely involves patience). And 8 years, to the date, He gives me a verse that says to "rejoice in the Lord," which automatically turns my mind to His character! No mistakes with God!! There will always be spiritual battles while we are here on this earth, but God's character will always remain the same! I am rejoicing in Him and loving that He knows how best to impact my heart and mind!!

"…rejoice in the Lord…"
Philippians 3:1

Amazing!

I was thinking this morning about how many people there are in this world! I know there are more than i can fathom. I know they exist, but, by *no* means, know them personally. Yet, how amazing is it to think of *all* the people in the world, in *all* the different places (even the most remote), doing *all* kinds of different things, touching *all* kinds of different lives, having *all* kinds of different cares and thrills, *all* with a specific part in God's overall plan!! And He knows *each* one of us by name! He knows *every* part of our lives! *Every* prayer that we make, He listens to, as though we were the only one around, and answers each one individually according to what is best!! It is so incredible to really think of *how much He loves and cares for us!!* Absolutely amazing!!

I know a lot of people. But by no means know everything about them–not even my closest friends. Because... there are thoughts that we would never share out loud. God knows those thoughts and loves us still. He sent His Son Jesus to the cross, knowing everything about the world He was dying for! He *still* chose to love us and offer His gift of salvation to us!! Again, i have to say, "How Amazing!!"

Counting Blessings

Pondering that though the Lord rarely takes me directly from point A to point B, there are so many blessings, and lessons, and people along the way that are important! I need to be quicker to be thankful and counting my blessings! I simply need to be joyful in the life He has planned specifically for me, to bring Him glory and honor!

Rejoicing

Though i don't understand or enjoy all the circumstances that this life brings my way, God tells me to, "Rejoice in Him always!" Philippians 4:4 That word "rejoice" comes from a Greek word, that means to be calmly happy. Makes me think it is really about resting in the Lord's character rather than being happy about the things going on around me. After all, either i believe God is sovereign or i don't. Let's be determined to "Rejoice in the Lord always!!"

Praise

Thinking about focusing on praising the Lord and bringing Him honor with the words that come out of my mouth. When i do that, there won't be a chance for my thoughts and words to be something they shouldn't be. Besides that, the Lord is worthy of my praise! He deserves glory!

Who Am I Praising?

Psalm 118:28 says, "Thou art my God, and I will praise Thee: Thou art my God, I will exalt Thee." As i read that, the first thought was that i am to praise and exalt the Lord, and i am! But then as i read it again, it came to mind that the one that i praise, and the one i exalt, is the one who is the focus of my life...who is that? Others--friends, family, kids? Myself? God? Whose praises am i known for voicing? Who am i lifting up on a daily basis in my life? That is who my God is! It makes me realize that it is so important to be sure i am lifting up and praising the one true God!! I don't want anyone to make any mistake about who the God i worship is!

A Grateful Heart vs. A Whining Spirit

My quiet time this morning was about being grateful to the Lord. It makes me think about the verse that says to give thanks in everything. The Lord does not have to bless me or love me or do anything good for me! He however chooses to do so because He is an amazing God! So...this morning i am cleaning because my house is in desperate need. And while i am tempted to whine about having to clean, the Lord reminds me to be grateful. He helps me rather to have His perspective-- i can be thankful that:

-i have a house to clean,

-the ability to do so,

-the time to do it,

-a vacuum that works,

-and a washer and dryer too...

ALL blessings that i don't always think about. So, i am going to do my best to be grateful for whatever this day holds.

The Goal of Praise

Thinking this morning that there are a lot of things i make an effort to do...such as laundry, dishes, housecleaning, visiting people, going to church, keeping up with friends and family, having a quiet time, grocery shopping...you get the idea...but the Bible says i am to praise the Lord and to sing praises to Him. It really is a joy to do that! He is merciful, and truthful, and always dependable!! But still it does take an effort to actually praise Him. The great part in that is that i can praise Him while i do those other things! What a wonderful place to put my efforts! What a good goal for my day!

Praising the Lord--Obviously

As my current prescription of glasses is broken and i am using ones 4 years old, i have had to be creative with my quiet time. No glasses makes the font in my Bible very difficult to read. So, since i have journaled over the years, i have been going back through some of what i have written (because i write much larger than the print in my Bible). Today i came across some notes on Psalm 150--which is all about praising the LORD! And i realize that we are to praise Him for Everything and Everywhere! We are also to do it on instruments and in dance--which means by implication, that we are to do it loudly and obviously! Everything that has breath is to praise the Lord!!

If i am praising

the God of the universe!

who is in control of all things!

and loves me more than anyone else could ever love me!

My focus needs to cease to be about me, or the worries i carry, or anything that would draw my focus somewhere else. This little Psalm is only 6 verses long but has so much impact if i will obey what it says!!

God Is Still Faithful and I Need to Be Grateful

I am reminded this morning about the little things that i don't always think about. Like having my prescription reading glasses...they broke yesterday and now reading is uncomfortable...sad about that especially when it comes to reading my Bible with an old prescription--that makes it very difficult to focus...and it will be over a week before they can be replaced...but still God is faithful and i need to be grateful! So, here's to knowing God's timing is still perfect and resting there. But how excited i will be to be able to read my Bible again with ease!

Quicker to Share God's Praise!

I am thinking this morning about how quick we are to share prayer requests (and that is so amazing to be able to do that!)...but how often are we quick to share praises with each other? These verses say to forget not all His benefits. And I am thinking the best way to remember something is repetition. So, for me, my goal today, is to share my praises with those I have contact with!

"Bless the LORD, O my soul: and all that is within me, bless His holy name.
Bless the LORD, O my soul, and forget not all His benefits:"
Psalm 103:1-2

What Praising God Is Not

This morning i read 2 different Psalms that were all about praising the Lord--no matter where you are, no matter what part of God's creation you are, and no matter when it is. It also talked about singing God's praise! And the thought comes to me that if i am praising the Lord, then i am:

Not complaining,

Not worrying,

Not stressing,

Not angry/mad,

Not getting even,

Not being hateful,

Not over-thinking things...

because all those focus on me.

But when i am praising the Lord, i am focusing on WHO HE IS!! What an amazing way to spend each and every day!!

Looking for God's Blessings and Praising Him for Them

Thinking that we are characterized by those things we "practice" often...and as i read scripture, there are those who are mentioned who obey the Lord and that He blesses. But there are others who obey and when the Lord blesses, you read about how they praise Him! I want to be like the latter ones. It seemingly doesn't take any effort to complain. It must not because we are so quick to do so. But what a wonderful place to put my efforts and energy into...praising my Lord and Savior!! After all He blesses constantly! He really does! How much am i willing to look for it, and have eyes that are quick to see it? Rejoicing and speaking of the works of the Lord is what i want to be 'practicing'

Thankfulness Rather Than Complaining

Thinking this morning about the ease and wealth with which we live! We know we have much and are blessed! Yet we are so thankless and ungrateful...always thinking about what we don't have or still want. How disappointing it must be at times to God! So, my goal for today is that every time i worry about something or complain, i need to verbalize 2 things i am thankful for and give God praise!! It is very convicting when i think of how easy we have it here on so many levels!

Praising the Lord Needs to Be More the Norm

"...come, let us declare in Zion the work of the LORD our God."
Jeremiah 51:10b

As i was reading this morning, and came to this verse, the Holy Spirit wouldn't let me go further. He reminded me that often we are quite quick to ask for people to pray. We are also very prone to vent and complain about God's timing and ways conflicting with our own. But how often do we share the answers to prayer when He gives them?? Or even something we didn't take the time to pray about, but we see and know it is the hand of God at work? I am convicted this morning that praising the Lord needs to be more of the norm for us, who are Christians...maybe even when it may not be what we hoped for but are trusting that the Lord knows best. God is good ALL the time!! Why not talk about it a little bit- no, a lot more often!

God on the Throne of My Life

Thinking that the one i am most concerned about being praised, is the one who is on the throne of my life...it should be the Lord! but sometimes it takes specific effort to make sure i am not more concerned about my own praise than i am about His...HE is the One who is worthy of all praise and glory!!

Reflecting God The Father, Son, And Holy Ghost

"2012"

As i sit here typing, i wonder what the Lord has done in and through me during this past year…sometimes i can be so positive and keep my eyes fixed on Him, but then there are those times when i have lost the proper focus and allowed my worries and anxieties to get the better of me. How frustrated i would think the Lord would get with me, yet He keeps right in there, working to draw me back to Himself. Loving me, caring for me, so far, far beyond what i deserve! I am so very very thankful for His forgiveness and constant love! Where would i be without it?? I shudder to think! I rarely see the good in myself, but whenever there is a glimpse, i know all the glory belongs to Him! This year my spiritual goal for the year was to "listen." More of a challenge for some of us than others. But i trust that most days i worked at listening to the Lord, whether through the loud voices of someone else or the still soft voice of His Holy Spirit. I find myself a bit melancholy this last day of 2012 but am still purposely resting in the fact that the Lord has a purpose in every year and every day of the lives of His children! "Thank You Lord for the year of 2012, and for what You have accomplished, and for the lessons learned! May they stick with me, and may i always be pliable in Your hands, trusting Your plan is always best!" May i "hang my hat there!" May the Lord lead you as you leave this year, taking with you the lessons learned, and leaving the problems in His hands, and press on to what He has for you in 2013!

Examples

As a mom of grown children, i don't often think of needing to be an example anymore…but the truth is that there is always someone who is watching me (us). I was reading my Bible this morning, and was impressed with the fact, that most children follow their parents' example. Sometimes it is consciously, and sometimes subconsciously. But they do, and there is no getting around it.

So, am i responsible for my grown children's actions? No, they make their own decisions. But i am responsible for how i live my own life, and the impact that it may have on someone else. The verse comes to mind that says we are to be an example to others in word and deed. The other thing that came to mind was, "What kind of example am i still setting for my kids as they watch the way i do things? Does what i say match what i do?" I guess it challenges me to remember that my life never impacts just me...so what kind of example *am* i living? By God's grace, i want to be an example to others in a way that brings honor and glory to Him! So thankful that what He wants me to do, He will enable me to do as well!

What Kind of Infuser?

As i have been reading through 1 Kings, there are many kings and some prophets that are written about. All of them, known for a certain kind of character. And all bearing certain consequences because of their character. I want to have godly character. But to think that my character, no matter what kind it is, affects only me, is simply ignorant. Quite a while back, the Lord brought to mind that my life is like an infuser. Consequently, it can infuse the area around me with the sweet aroma of His character.

Counting My Blessings

Trusting Him

Resting In Him. Praying

Studying His Word

Kindness, Mercy And Grace

Putting God First

Loving Others

These things infuse the air around me with a sweet smell. But only being surrendered to the Lord will bring this kind of "infusing."

On the flip side, have you ever smelled a candle or infuser that just does not smell so good? The analogy works that way too– if my life is filled with selfishness, worry, complaining, materialism, stress, gossip, choosing to be ignorant, harshness, and revenge, then the air around me will, quite simply put, *s t i n k*. And honestly, apart from the Lord, those are all my natural tendencies.

I want to be so in tune to the Lord, that the "air around me" smells sweetly of His character because i am allowing Him to be the oil that infuses me, to then share the sweet aroma with those around me. Here's to a day, for us all, that is a little sweeter smelling, for us and those around us, than some days tend to be.

Truth Does Not Change

I have been thinking this morning about how the American culture has a silly notion, that because we have the freedom to believe what we want to, then we are all right. If people really thought that through, they would realize how illogical that is! As our pastor says, we can disagree and both be wrong, but we cannot disagree and both be right. As i was reading this morning in Revelation, i was reminded that God is KING OF KINGS AND LORD OF LORDS. And that is exactly how it was written (all in capital letters). Several things come immediately to mind. One is that He has always been KING OF KINGS AND LORD OF LORDS, and *He always will be!* You can believe it or not, but it does not change the truth of it. And the Bible tells us that one day, *every* knee will bow before Him, both in Heaven and in earth! He *will* get the honor He is worthy of! How wonderful it will be to be able to worship Him fully, as He deserves! :D The other thing is that, i personally, am challenged to yield my thoughts, and my words, and my actions to Him, in such a way that others will see the testimony that i *really do believe,* that He is KING OF KINGS AND LORD OF LORDS!! I was never put here to bring attention or glory to myself, but to the One who saved me and is worthy of my life's devotion. And i want to (by His grace and strength) bring Him glory 24/7. A challenge i want to always be working at. ;)

Reflecting Christ Rather Than Self

Thinking about the definition of grace, according to Strong's Concordance-- the Divine influence upon the heart, reflected in the life...makes me wonder what influence others see in me...is it Divine or just mine? 2 Peter 3:18 says to grow in grace, and in the knowledge of our Lord and Savior, Jesus Christ...only as i know Him more, will i reflect Him more. They go hand in hand.

Time with God Changes Perspective

Thinking this morning that it makes such a difference to start each day sitting down with the Lord!! And i don't always realize the impact it makes til i hear from someone who is struggling, and has not gotten to know the Lord, and His love, and His character, over the years. It affects my perspective, my attitude, and my actions. If not for the Lord...so thankful that He has grown me over the years, much of that through trials. But as i know Him more, i love Him more, and see things through His eyes more. So glad i will always have room to grow this side of Heaven!

Encouraging?

I want to be someone who is helpful. I also want to be encouraging those i know, in the right direction (God's direction)...and always in love--the way the Heavenly Father encourages me to do what is right...

"Iron sharpens iron, so a man sharpens the countenance of his friend."
Proverbs 27:17

Receiving Generosity Should Result in Being Generous

Thinking on God's generosity to all of His children.... not only do i need to be more grateful, but that i need to strive to be more like Him...therefore generous to others...and that does not always mean monetarily. Sometimes it means generous with my time, or generous with a sweet spirit, or with a listening ear, or to lend a hand, and the list can go on. But the point is to be generous. And also, when it comes to being grateful...God really has given us all so much!! I am afraid that especially we Americans get so comfortable in our abundance that we forget we should be thanking God, and not just thinking we are supposed to have all that we do! God does not have to bless! He could give us what we deserve.... But He is gracious and generous instead!

A Man After God's Own Heart

As i was reading this morning about King David and his compassion on his son, Absalom (who was wanting to take the throne from him), i was reminded of the fact that God called David a man after His own heart. David didn't want anyone to harm Absalom, in spite of all he was doing against him. And when he was killed, the king was heartbroken, and wished it had been him! Compassion, mercy, forgiveness, unconditional love! All are descriptive of how David's heart was like God's...and i want to have a heart like that as well! Which means, it needs to be that way, in spite of how others may act or feel towards me. But i also stop and think about the fact that that is how God treats me!! How amazing His love toward His children really is!!!

Thankfulness

Thinking that as i go through my day and do the many things that need to be done, i want to remember to be thankful that i am able to do them. There are those i visit who are unable to do the things they used to not even have a second thought about...so much i take for granted. Thank you, Lord, for my health and ability!

All About Perspective

Some mornings it is a little more of a challenge to have a thankful spirit, but the Bible says in everything to give thanks...so i am thankful for the fact that though the Lord has called me to visit older people, who can't get out, and they end up going to be with Him, that He blessed me with knowing them, and i will see them again one day. I am also thankful that the Lord is my refuge and strength. I am thankful that, though the chore of grocery shopping needs to be done (and i don't always like doing it), He has blessed me with the funds to do so. It is all about perspective. So i am thanking the Lord that He gives me His perspective in place of mine.

All Things Pleasing to the Lord

Thinking this morning that i want the things i do and the thoughts i have, to please the Lord, whether it be in the ordinary or the out of the ordinary...all of it should be for Him!

Influence?

Thinking this morning that we all have influence on someone, probably several "someones"...so is my influence pleasing to the Lord, or am i using it for selfish reasons? Especially as women, i think we carry more influence on more people than we realize at times...pondering...

What Kind of Tone Setter Am I?

This morning i am thinking about the fact, that as a woman, i tend to set the tone for my home...so what kind of tone am i setting? I want to be a reflection of Christ in all i do...so the question is, if i were to ask those closest to me (those who are in and out of my home on a regular basis), "What kind of tone do i set," what would they say? Just my ponderings this morning.

Reflecting Christ

They say the longer you are married the more like each other you become. Then, i think about the fact that marriage is a picture of Christ and the church. So, it stands to reason, that the longer i am a child of God, the more like Him i should become. I am called to be obedient to Him. To do that, i must know Him (by reading His Word, and listening, and talking with Him). I want to know Him so well and love Him so much that it comes more and more naturally to obey Him and to be like Him...

Infused with God

Thinking this morning that i want to be so infused with God that His thoughts and attitudes fill my thoughts and attitudes! To do that i must be reading my Bible and getting to know who God really is. And i also must be surrendered to His leading and direction. It takes work and deliberation.

God Is the One Who Needs to be Seen Not Me

Thinking that it is Not important that others see how strong i am, but rather see God's strength, regardless of my strength or weakness. God is the One deserving of all glory and honor!! And if there is any true strength in me, then it comes from Him!

More Like Jesus

Thinking this Wednesday morning that my sin never just affects myself. My thoughts and actions always affect someone else. And the Holy Spirit brings to mind that this should inspire me to be more and more like Jesus! After all, i am to love Him with every part of my being. The more you love someone and the more you spend time with them, the more like them you become! Sounds like an awesome goal for my day!

Reflecting Christ

Thinking this morning that when others look at me or think of me, i want them to see Christ, and not just me...that does require me to be focused and diligent in my walk with Him, on a daily basis!

Loving Him, listening to Him, following Him, and relying on Him.

Bringing Glory to God

Pondering this morning that God's opinion of me is more important than anyone else's! But He desires for me to bring Him glory, and part of doing that, is to live in a way that others see Him in me...wanting my life to count for my Savior and Lord!

What Does My Walk Look Like?

Pondering this morning as i continue to read through 2 Kings, about many of the different kings of Judah and Israel...it often refers to how they followed in the ways of the Lord or in the ways of the previous king. And it makes me do a bit of a self-examination as to what it would look like if someone followed after my ways...just my thoughts for today.

Glorifying God

Thinking that, contrary to popular opinion, we are not here to serve and entertain ourselves, but rather to bring glory to the Lord and to serve Him and others ...not exactly our natural instinct, but it IS worth the cost!

I Belong to Jesus, Am I Living for Him?

A day of introspection--am i really giving myself entirely to what the Lord wants me to? To Himself? I belong to Him and am here to do His will. If i look at it through the world's eyes, it is a bit of a chore and a bore. But as His child, i know it is not that way at all. He loves me more than i can imagine! And to love Him back and to live my life to bring Him glory, actually brings blessings, and peace, and contentment, like nothing else.

What is On My Mind?

Adjusting My Attitude

Pondering the fact that it is a blessing that the Lord allows me a certain amount of ignorance when it comes to His plans. I am afraid that if i knew all the details of His purposes, i would either try to eliminate some of it or speed it up. So glad that His ways and timing are perfect...now to adjust my attitude accordingly, on a day by day basis--this is the challenge.

Actively Taking Thoughts Captive

I am thinking that to allow the Lord to take every thought captive, takes me being sensitive to the Holy Spirit's leading. Responding in obedience takes action. It is not a passive sort of thing.

God's Perspective

Thinking this morning about the fact that in Psalm 119, the Psalmist asks God for understanding of His Word. And i realize that, at times, it is easy to assume that i will know what God means, or wants me to walk away with, from a certain portion of scripture. But it is so much better to ask Him to make it clear to me. Because above all, i want to truly understand His Word and His perspective. It is having the mindset that it is more important that i ask the Lord to help me deal with each day, with His attitude, and looking through the eyes of His truth, rather than to always be asking for Him to change my circumstances. That is the only way i will be more like Him and what He wants me to be. Besides which one of us enjoys being misquoted or misunderstood? My food for thought...

Controlling Thoughts

Thinking this morning about a couple of verses..."Let the words of my mouth and the meditation of my heart be acceptable in Thy sight, O Lord, my strength and my redeemer." Psalm 19:14 "For out of the abundance of the heart the mouth speaks." Luke 6:45 I have been thinking this weekend about how important it is that i can control my thoughts. Because my thoughts are what tend to come out in my words, and attitudes/emotions, and actions. It is so important that i see this life through God's truth and His perspective!! It really does affect soooo much!

"What's on Your Mind?"

This is the question the Lord has brought to my mind. Well, this morning it is the fact that sometimes i allow too much to be on my mind. Instead, i should let the Lord have those things, and find my peace and refuge in Him. I need to stop trying to find security in having some sort of “control” over things that are not mine to control anyway. How important it is to rest in the Lord and just really trust Him with EvErYtHiNg! No matter the size!

What Am I Feeding My Mind?

Thinking this morning that unfortunately, it is not hard to be critical of someone else and how they have acted or spoken or a bad attitude they have had. But the truth is that what is on my mind comes from whatever i am "feeding" it. So, are the things i am nourishing my mind with pleasing to the Lord? Are the things i spend time pondering things that would honor Him? Because what honors Him is also good for me.

Pondering the Goodness of God

Goal for today-- to set my mind to pondering the amazing love of God that He shows me in so many different ways! He has given me my salvation first and foremost! He has blessed me with a wonderful husband and family. He has given sunshine and rain to bring about the springtime that i thoroughly enjoy! He even gives me bad days to remind me that my joy comes from Him and not my circumstances. It is a good thing to make a list every once in a while to remind myself of His goodness!

Variety...Good or Bad?

Thinking that variety can be sort of nice. There is so much variety in who God is! There will never be enough time in this lifetime to think on all of who God is! But one must beware because there is also much that can draw someone away from Jesus and the truths of His Word!

His Blessings

Excelling at Thankfulness

As i read in Colossians this morning, i stopped at chapter 2, verses 6 and 7. I wrote them out and looked up the original Greek meanings of some of the words to get a more in depth idea of what they were intended to communicate. So i am going to paraphrase it accordingly. . . As you have received Christ Jesus the Lord, live *a life conformed* to the union entered into with Him: Having an *established communion with Christ,* and *growing in your spiritual life.* Also *be steadfast (unmovable) in your fellowship with Christ. Don't let anything come between you and Him.* And be *always increasing in your excellence of giving thanks to God for His blessings...* it is the last phrase that jumps out at me. I have been a Christian now (in 2012) for 44 years, and i am always learning and growing! Sometimes more painfully than others. Because that is the case, not only do i need to be firm in living my life consistent with what i believe, i.e. reflecting Christ, and spending time with Him, at least daily, but i need to be excelling at giving Him thanks for His blessings!! If you know me personally, you know i try to be optimistic, more often than pessimistic. But the thought of becoming more and more excellent at giving thanks to the Lord, as a part of growing in Him, puts a little more of a twist on it (at least in my way of thinking). So, it is no longer just a personality trait or something that i am supposed to do to please Him, but it is a reflection of my growth in Him. I am definitely challenged to become more excellent at giving thanks to the Lord for His many blessings! After all, He doesn't have to bless me at all! But He does it because He loves me!! So, here's to all of us becoming better and better at not just noticing God's blessings but thanking Him for them.

A Good Day

It has been a good day. But nothing out of the ordinary. I read my Bible, made a menu and went grocery shopping, came home and put away groceries, did dishes and watched a little tv But that is okay. Funny how sometimes we (at least i) think it has to be exciting or different, to be a day we would talk about to others. But i am thinking that if someone were to ask how my day was, i would probably say "okay, nothing unusual." But how about saying instead, "It has been a good day -- nothing has gone wrong, and i am content...hmm...what a blessing it is to just be content!" Yes! I think that is both truthful and encouraging. I believe the Lord wants me to be both those things. I hope you are having a good day– whatever is happening! And that whether it is exciting or maybe even a bit boring, that you can rejoice because you have learned to be content.

God...Our Best Source (for 2013)

As this new year begins, i know that many of us may be hoping for fewer struggles and better things or times than we had last year. And maybe we even want to leave some of the past year behind...so as i write this, that is sort of the background of my thoughts. It seems like i would love to grow in the Lord, without growing pains. But the truth is, that rarely happens. It just does not have the same results when i think i can "do things on my own," rather than having to depend on God! So i am thinking about how He wants us to deal with the trials He puts in our lives. He wants to make us more like Himself. There are so many promises He gives in His Word. They are not there to take up pages, but to encourage us as His children! I am so very thankful for that!! His mercies are new every morning! *His grace is sufficient (it is not almost enough, but MORE than enough)!* He will guide my steps, but also reign me in, if that is what i need! *No one can pluck me from, or pry me out of His hands!* I am safe and secure in His loving care! *He is patient and understanding (even when i am not).*

He is the perfect Father! *He is Lord of the universe, and there is nothing beyond His control or reach!* He loves us perfectly! *He is our Rock (our stability)!* He is our refuge and strength! *He never casts us off or forsakes us!*

I notice that none of these things have to do with who or what i am, but everything to do with who God is!! Honestly, i may know some of what some of you are struggling with, but most of you i do not. So, by no means, am i pointing this at anyone. Many times, i am easily distracted from where my focus should be. But the Lord really impressed on me this morning, that there were several who could benefit from the encouragement He gave me today. So, may you be encouraged by the words that turn our hearts and minds to the One who has all of our lives in His care! He loves us so much more than we can ever fathom!! May He lift your spirits and give you the peace that goes beyond our own understanding!

Gifts

As i look back to the Sunday morning sermon this past week, i am remembering that the pastor said that as we give gifts to others, we need to remember the greatest gift of all that we have in God sending His Son! And my mind starts to go a little farther with that…the first thing that comes to mind is that God gave great thought in the gift He gave! It was sacrificial, on so many levels!! For Christ to come spend 30 plus years on this sinful earth, where people would falsely accuse Him and eventually crucify Him! What a gift! Not only on Jesus' part, but on God the Father's, as well! It was a very high price He paid for that first Christmas gift! But because of the love He has for us, He never batted an eye. I am so grateful! Then, i think of how we wrap our gifts when we give them. Jesus did not come in some "royal" way but humbly, to a humble home, born in a barn and wrapped in swaddling clothes. It was not to bring attention on a grand scale (Though it was very grand to the shepherds!!)! And it is the most amazing gift ever to those of us who are His children!! But it demonstrates humility and love! And the other thing i am thinking is, that in our family, my husband and i love to give gifts (when the finances allow). We love to come up with ideas that will be pleasing to others. It *is* a blessing to give! And i know that the Lord loves us even more than we love each other!! So i am going to concentrate today on paying attention to and being grateful for, the *many* gifts the Lord gives me on a daily basis!!

Today i am thankful that God has given us the gift of laughter. It lightens my spirits and makes me smile!

Thinking on the joy that comes from fellowship with my Lord and Savior--there is nothing to compare!

Declaring God's Working

Thinking this morning that as a child of the King, i should be declaring how He works in my life, on a daily basis. He is always blessing us (me). But do i take the time to stop and thank Him? Or pay attention? If i were checking out of a store, would i thank a clerk for checking me out and tell her to have a nice day...that is just being polite. If someone were to give me something or do something special just for me, i would be appreciative and tell them, "Thank you so much!" And i might even go tell others how nice these people were to me. But God does things for me, materially, emotionally, and spiritually, on a constant basis! How often do i tell Him "Thank you," on the spot?! Or go and tell others what He has done for me? So, don't they tell us the best time to start is now? Today, already, (it's 9:30 a.m. that i am writing this) i have been blessed! I woke up and was able to move around...i didn't need help walking or getting where i wanted to be. I was a little stiff, but it reminds me to be thankful that it is not always the case. I had a little bit of a conversation with my son before he left for work. My husband and i have chatted. And i even chatted with my sister-in-law online. The Lord has blessed me with family that i love, and that love me, and that love Him! I do understand that not all families are like that. He also gave me time to spend with Him! That is the best part of my day, hands down!! Time when He reminds me of who He is, and things i need to be doing- things that are pleasing to Him and bring Him glory. He was specifically reminding me of His love this morning! How amazing it is! Even though it is undeserved, He gives it freely!! He is worthy of my worship and praise--daily, and moment by moment! Not just around Thanksgiving, but all year long! I want to be quicker to declare His works! I want to be thankful and voice my praise and thanks to Him! Others may see a difference in me, but if i never share what makes that difference, how will they know?!

Blessings

Thinking there are so many blessings associated with being a part of God's family...do i take advantage of them? Do i accept the joyous responsibility of being interconnected with others??

The Blessing of Trials

Thinking that we do not look at the trials of this life as enjoyable. What we need is to see them from God's perspective. They are a part of life so that we can see God work and watch how faithful He is during the hard times. They can actually be a blessing because we are looking to see what He will do.

God's Generosity

Thinking that i need to be more aware of the generosity of my Lord and Savior! Not just in physical ways, but also spiritual and emotional ways. The ways that cannot possibly be measured because they are beyond measure! Things like peace and contentment! His Holy Spirit leading and guiding my thoughts and desires! Thank you, Jesus!!

God's Blessings/ Peace

As i ponder on God's word this morning, i am thinking about the many blessings He gives on a daily basis! He doesn't have to, but He does it anyway. Sometimes to honor our obedience and reverence of Him. I have learned much of His character over the years! Though at times, my thoughts and plans might not have been His. His ways are always a blessing to me, when i am willing to look at life through His perspective. And i do believe one of the most significant blessings He gives is that of peace and contentment. It is a void only He can fill!! The world looks to fill that void in so many ways. But there is nothing they can obtain or do that will give a lasting peace and contentment like what God gives! There is just nothing like it!! To Him be the glory!!

God's Blessings

Thinking today that God blesses us all with so many things! He is full of goodness and blessing! But when i complain and gripe, more than i praise and thank Him, who is getting the glory? Not the Lord! In fact, i would say it is our enemy the devil. God is victorious in all things! So i need to be sure that that is how i live my life and use my words! Even if it doesn't look like He is blessing, i can trust

His heart and know that He is!! Hope you all are able to take time to look for and notice the goodness and blessings from our Lord and Savior!!

Blesser and Deliverer

Thinking this morning, as i look down at this sweet little bundle of joy i have been blessed with in my grandson, that there are many blessings that the Lord gives us! But He also gives trials in our lives to keep us mindful that He is not only the giver of all that is good, but He is also our deliverer! He never gives up on His children or gives us more than He can handle for us! There is much beyond our ability, but nothing beyond His!

Aware of God's Blessings

Thinking about how important it is to be thankful this morning! So many blessings the Lord has given me!! And so many He continuously gives on a daily basis! Being more aware and more thankful...the goal for my day. It might do me (and us all) some good to make a list of all that He blesses me with. Maybe even keep it where it is handy and available to look at on my bad days.

Blessing of God's Word in My Language

Thinking that i am so very thankful for God's Word!! I cannot even imagine living somewhere where i did not have it in my own language! We are so blessed here to have the ability and the freedom to read it!!! How awful it must be to be otherwise!

Paying Attention to God's Goodness

Pondering this morning how we say God is good all the time, but sometimes don't quite believe it like we should...but honestly, only in Him and His ways, will there ever be lasting joy, contentment and peace!! And i need to remember that His "good" is so far beyond my personal mentality of good!! Going to set my goal today for paying attention in a major way to His goodness!!

Seeing the Blessings When I am Willing to Look

Often i hear the statement that God is good all the time. But more times than not, it is when He has answered "yes" to our prayers...but this morning i am thinking that God really is good ALL the time! Even when He doesn't answer our prayers or desires the way we would like. This morning it is pretty cold outside! And it is definitely warmer inside my house than out there! But the truth is--that my attitude has everything to do with a perspective that God gives, and not so much with my circumstances! I am thinking this morning about the fact that our furnace has been on the fritz since before Thanksgiving (It needs to be replaced). It can be run for short amounts of time but does not work to the fullest and we have been told that there could be an issue of CO2 in the air, so to be very careful. Needless to say, we have not run it very much. When we do run it, it doesn't do much more than slightly take the chill off the air. But you know what? I am so thankful for the things that i do have! Things like jeans and big bulky sweaters, for blankets and afghans, and a couple of space heaters. I am thankful for my waterbed (because it is heated). I am grateful for hot food, for hot chocolate, for coffee for my guys, and for hot tea for me. I am thankful for kitty cats to sit in my lap and keep me (and them) warm. I really appreciate a hot shower! And i am thankful that God helps me to see the blessings when i am willing to look! He IS good all the time! Sometimes i think we just need to be willing to see it. Thanks be to Him for all His blessings that He gives all the time!!

Living in the "Now"

Thinking this morning that there is much i look back on with gratitude to the Lord and much i anticipate that He will do in the future! And that is good. But what about today? Am i looking at the blessings of the moment, here and now? God doesn't want me missing what He is doing now because i am too focused elsewhere... so here's to a day of counting my current blessings and seeing what God is doing now!

Prayer

Hopeful or Worrisome?

Thinking this morning that the Lord has blessed me with a burden to pray for others. And i am so thankful for the opportunity to take my cares for them to the One who is Almighty and Victorious! But i must confess that, at times, my care and concern for them can turn to worrying, if i am not careful. As i was reading in my Bible this morning, i read some verses that reminded me that the Lord calls me to do certain things. Beyond that however, i MUST TRUST HIM for the results. After all GOD is:

ALMIGHTY	GRACIOUS	GLORIOUS
VICTORIOUS	MERCIFUL	AMAZING
ALL- POWERFUL	ALL-SEEING	AWESOME
LOVING	ALL-KNOWING	FORGIVING
SOVEREIGN	GREAT	

He is God, and there is none like Him! Prayer is a privilege! But when it is trimmed in worry, i miss the peace of casting all my cares on Him because He cares for me! I am so grateful that His "eyesight" and His ability are not limited like mine! A song comes to mind that says, "I am resting in the joy of who God is!" I would quote it, but i can't quite remember it word for word. The idea is that i am to rest in the person of Jesus Christ and love finding out who He is and the greatness of His loving heart! To do that is so much better than basing my faith and hopes on my limited "line of vision" and lack of ability. So...here's to praying with the confidence in who God is!! Have a wonderful day!!

Praying in Faith

It is one thing to pray and worry about how and when God will answer. It is quite another to pray and to watch expectantly and thankfully because you are confident that the Lord is going to answer according to what is best and in the best time.

Pray-Yes, Worry-No

Thinking that i cannot be responsible for someone else's actions. However, i must take responsibility for my own. The Lord calls me to be like Him. That means i must be in His Word listening to His still small voice speaking into my life and obey. But to worry about others is not what i am to do. Pray-yes, worry-no.

Importance of Prayer

I am thinking that we need to grasp how important prayer is, on so many levels!! It is what we are called to do moment by moment. It is wonderful to know that we can take our cares to the Lord at any time and that He will answer in the way that He knows is best. And that is a wonderful place to rest!

A Sweet Sound in God's Ears

" I love you, Lord,
And i lift my voice,
To worship You,
O my soul rejoice,
Take joy my King,
In what You hear,
May it be a sweet, sweet sound in Your ears."

Those are words to a song that is running through my head this morning. There have definitely been times when i have done nothing but whine to the Lord. Yet He loves me still, and He is patient with me. But i don't want my communication with Him, to be a constant whining and complaining sort of thing. I want it to be something we both enjoy!

Diligent in Prayer and Trusting the Lord

Thinking this morning that it is so important to keep on praying and to keep on hoping in the Lord! The devil would like to see us get discouraged. But God is God! So, there is no need to do that! He will answer in His perfect time and way. I must also remember that whatever the Lord does always affects others as well. His ways are so far beyond mine! The Bible says the effectual fervent prayer of a righteous man avails much! So, i need to remain diligent and keep trusting through the process. It is then that i will look forward to giving Him thanks and all the glory WHEN God brings the answer!

His Ways and Purpose

Is Friction Always Bad?

I am thinking about the things in the news that i wish were not...about how this country is no longer the religious and moral country it used to be. Those kinds of thoughts can bring a certain fear and panic, if i allow them to. But as the Lord usually does when i am willing to listen, He gives me more of His perspective than mine. I am so glad that He does!! He reminds me that beauty and strength do not come about from life being easy. When a bodybuilder is working at building his strength, he has to bear through the pain to get there. Consistency and endurance are definitely involved! When a diamond is found, it does not look like what we think of as a diamond. The rough exterior must be chipped away. Then, the different facets are cut into the stone before you see the sparkling rock we think of as a diamond. In the same way, precious metals must go through a refining fire to get rid of the imperfections. Only then do you see the real beauty that lies within. These things remind me that when life is too easy, there is not the beauty and strength that there could be. I look at our nation and think about how much freedom we have had over the years and how there are those who are trying to take it away, on numerous levels. But true to form, the Lord brings to my attention the verse that tells how Joseph told his brothers that even though they meant it for harm when they sold him, God meant it for good. Even though there was much that didn't seem good in that time in between, God had put him in a place and position to help keep his family alive! It is a fact that the church has grown more when it has been under persecution. So, while i have never been a glutton for punishment, if i want my family in Christ to grow, then i need to realize that some things are necessary. Don't get me wrong; i am not saying the things that are happening are wonderful. They are not! In fact- people are trying to squelch the truth of God's Word. I would never be in favor of that! But God is still God! And all that He does/allows has purpose! Good purpose for His children! No one has ever been able to completely do away with God's people or His Word! They have tried and never fully succeeded! And they won't! Friction, pain, and troubles are a necessary, refining part of life. So though i would like to have things stay as easy as they have been in the past, i must realize that if i want to be more like Christ, there must be those times of refining. I never want to lose sight of the fact that God is in full and total control!

Why??

Why me? Well, why not me? Isn't it better to go through things that are hard and unpleasant, if it means *i get to know the Lord better and on a more personal level*? Makes me think of the little saying that says, "A friend in need is a friend indeed." After the Bible study i went to last night and the reading i did this morning in Psalms, i am very aware of *how much better* i know the Lord because of the very hard times in my life. I have no desire to relive any of them. But the lessons i learned and the character of my Lord, that i know, on a personal level, deep in my heart because of them, i would not trade for anything!! Not anything in the world! The Lord never promised me that He would put me in some protective bubble that would keep me from any and all the bad things of this world. He actually promised the opposite–that there will be troubles and sufferings, but that He will be with me through them all and give the grace that i need to get through them! He promises that to all of His children! So i would like to share some of those characteristics of God that He has taught me, on a very personal level, over the years.

Through 15 months of waiting (we had moved to NC from NY, and were living with friends and house-sitting until our other home sold), He taught me His sovereignty–up close and personal. He met all our needs. He taught me to be still and to trust His ways and His timing! And it was perfect!

Through 2 years of depression, He showed me His faithfulness, in spite of my emotionally limited thought process. He also blessed me with the faithfulness of my dear husband who rose to the occasion, even when i didn't respond in a positive manner.

Through David's recovery from his major car accident, a few of the things were patience, focus on God's character, and His unchanging ways!

Through a very bad financial time, He once again provided our needs, inspired us to free ourselves from credit cards, and humbled us in a way we had never thought we had an issue with.

Then, when there were major problems within our family, the Holy Spirit brought me to pray fervently and to once again be still and watch what God would do! To honestly trust Him with those i love so much! And also watch as He drew them to Himself!

Some of you know these things about me…but it is always a good exercise when the Lord reminds me to focus on His character and the work He has done in the past! Makes me think of how He used to have the Israelites set up monuments in those places where He did specific things that He wanted them to remember and to tell the generations of people to come. He always has a purpose in my suffering–always for my good and for His glory! What a blessing to know He loves His children so much!! And to take the time to look back at what He has done and know that He will continue to work in me as long as i am here.

When Life Changes…

I have been thinking lately that the Lord has me at a different place in my life than i have ever been before. I have been babysitting out of my home for about the last 18 years, and He has made it clear that it is not something He wants me to do full time anymore...Wow! What a change! I *know* it is of Him. But now to figure out what it is He *does* want me to do with my days...don't get me wrong–there has been very little boredom. Projects could keep me busy for quite some time. In fact, that is what i started out doing. But as i was sitting talking to the Lord this morning and being a little impatient with wanting to know His direction, His response was to tell me He loved me, and He does have a purpose for me, and i need to be patient. I say all that to share that the Lord reminded me that He has always had a purpose for me even before i was born. How amazing is that (Psalm 139)!! And though i have an inkling of what it is He is wanting for me to do, i know that in His perfect time He *will* make it clear to me. And it will bring Him glory and accomplish a work that He has planned specifically for me to do, to honor Him. That is what i want to do! Sometimes it means leaving that comfort zone that we all create for ourselves. But honestly i must remember that it is not about what *i* can do! It is about being yielded to my Savior and letting Him do as He will through me. Life changes–often more than we would like. But it is in those times that we grow. And unlike society, that says beauty is all about being youthful, the Bible talks often about beauty in terms of character–and that comes through age and experience. I don't want to go back in time. I want to go forward, in order to become more and more like Christ, always willing to be pliable in His hands and trusting that His beauty will shine through me!

God's Ways vs. Man's Ways

So i am thinking this morning about a subject that most of us women bristle at...don't stop reading, please. Submission is a topic that most people don't approach these days. But the truth of the matter is, that God gave each of us *specific roles*. It does not mean we are inferior, but it does mean that we have different things God wants us to accomplish. He made the man to rule over his household and the woman to care for the household and be the nurturer. Have you ever worked under 2 bosses? My husband used to be a vendor and he had a company boss and a store boss, in every store he serviced. It was not always an easy job to please them all. Have we ever thought about the fact that the Lord is just trying to save us from grief? But i also know that the curse of sin brought with it a desire in women to want to rule over their husbands (Genesis 3:15). And most of us would attest to the fact that we like to be in charge. Well, guess what...God says we don't get to do that with our husbands (Ephesians 5:22-28). But we argue that "You just don't understand my situation." But i am thinking about the fact that this is not an argument with my husband (our husbands) this is an argument with God and His ways. The culture, in which we live, says we have rights. We need to be happy, we need________ (you can fill in the blank). But what a different place this would be if the husbands would cherish their wives and the wives would respect and submit to their husbands! The world wants you to believe differently. Yet what i know to be true, is that God's ways are best! With obedience to Him, comes peace and contentment. I didn't say it would be easy–and we ladies feel the need to use our daily amount of words, sometimes at our husbands' expense–but obedience to the Lord is always well worth it! Why not use those daily words to encourage our husbands!! If we women would respect and honor our husbands (yes that includes submission), we would find that they, in turn, would be much more loving and caring.

Paths

I have a picture in my mind today, that has a tight rope, a balance beam, and a wide dirt path. The first thing i see is a tightrope–definitely not stable! And a fall is a l-o-n-g way down…this is the path i see when my plans and directions are all my own or about me. It just does not work well! The next thing is a balance beam–a little more stable, but still a fall or a stumble can be pretty severe…that is the path that has me in charge, but i am relying on friends to help me along. The problem here is that i will disappoint my friends and vice versa. We are fallible and there is no getting around it. And when i am relying on a friend to do what i should be relying on God to do, friendships are often damaged. The last path i see is that broad dirt path. That is the path God has laid out for me. It is wide and stable, because it is based on *His* truth, *His* ways, *His* attitude, *His* character, *His* love, and *His* direction. *In HIM there is stability and safety!!* It doesn't mean that nothing can or will cross our paths, but we can be sure-footed when we are abiding in Him! And as we follow His leading in our lives, may we be sure to give Him the praise for keeping us from slipping! To Him be the glory!! May we all have a "sure-footed" weekend!

"You enlarged my path under me; so my feet did not slip."
2 Samuel 22:37

Who Am I Fighting?

It is so important that i realize the fact that i am not to be in a battle with any other person! My battle on this earth is one against the forces of evil! The parts of the armor of God that He tells us to put on are not anything that would hurt a person, in fact quite the opposite! But they definitely will defeat the forces of evil! One of Satan's tools is division.

Do i really want to give him that kind of foothold? Absolutely not! So, here's to a day of wearing truth, righteousness, the gospel of peace, faith, salvation, the Word of God, prayer, perseverance, and supplication! So that the forces of evil will not be able to penetrate, and so that there will not be divisions among us!

"For we wrestle not against flesh and blood, but against principalities, against powers, against the rulers of the darkness of this world, against spiritual wickedness in high places. Wherefore take unto you the whole armor of God, that ye may be able to withstand in the evil day, and having done all, to stand [not attack]. Stand therefore, having your loins girt about with truth, and having on the breastplate of righteousness, and your feet shod with the preparation of the gospel of peace; above all taking the shield of faith, wherewith ye shall be able to quench [put out] all the fiery darts of the wicked. And take the helmet of salvation, and the sword of the Spirit, which is the word of God: praying always with all prayer and supplication in the Spirit, and watching thereunto with all perseverance and supplication for all saints."

Ephesians 6:12-18

Life Like a Puzzle

Thinking this morning (because i love puzzles) about how this life reminds me of a giant puzzle--a masterpiece that God has created. He knows exactly where the pieces fit and which ones need to go in first. Unfortunately, i can get so distracted by the one piece that i either can't find or that i want to put in, and it won't fit. When i do that, i forget that His "puzzle" IS beautiful! But i must understand that He knows which ones need to come first!! His "puzzle" is like the ones that contain many smaller pictures, that then, when put together, create His BeAuTiFuL work of art!!

God's Plan for Me

Thinking that since the Lord has a purpose, specific for each of us, and everyone is equal in His eyes, i need to be content to be where He has me. I need to be doing what He has me doing--and not get caught up in the process of comparing myself, in any way, to anyone else. God did not create us to be someone else!

Timing

So often i want to know when the Lord is going to put things together. Is He going to "fix" something? But what i should be doing, is trusting Him and using my energy to go about doing those things that are pleasing to Him. I need to be looking at His character, not just what He is doing.

Spiritual Gifts

My thoughts this morning.... that comparing where God has gifted me and called me to where He has called and gifted others is rarely helpful. In fact, at times, it makes me disobedient and unproductive. God's calling in each of our lives is different, and that is what is best. Whether someone has a gift that everyone sees, or that hardly anyone sees, or whether they are busy with it all the time, or they don't have the opportunity to use it every moment of every day...what is most important is that i be sensitive to what it is the Lord wants me to do and when. Just to rejoice that He wants to use me to do His work! That is a much better perspective (i speak from experience)!!

God's Yoke Not Mine

There always seems to be some sort of burden i can carry--whether for me or for someone else. But the truth of the matter is that God is the One who can carry it best! He is able to do so much more than i can think or imagine (Matthew 11:30)!!

Distraction vs Purpose

There are so many distractions that this world offers us. I am thinking about the fact that they are not necessarily bad in and of themselves, but when they become what we look for on a consistent basis, there is very little contentment or satisfaction. As i sit thinking this morning, i realized that when "distraction" is what my life is about, the balance is very off kilter. God did *not* plan for my life to be just random stuff, filling my days. He is not random. Everything He does has purpose (even when we don't see it). There are obligations i have chosen in my life, but when i start looking for distractions, those things cease to be accomplished like the Lord would have them to be. As i thought about these things, the commandments that God called the greatest came to mind. To love the Lord your God with all that you are! And to love your neighbor as yourself! In other words, i need to be sure God and people are my first priority, and in that order. When they are, then i will be both obedient and content. I will be honest with you...lately, i have lacked direction. But as i ponder it, i realize that i have been looking for those distractions, rather than for what it is the Lord wants me to do with my days. I do belong to Him! And by experience, i know that i am happiest when i am walking according to His will and surrendering my days to Him. There are specific things i *know* He wants me to do, and those should be my first concern. When i need a break, He will provide it. I just need to be careful not to throw the scale off balance with "distractions." So here is to a better focus and direction!

Content in Who God Made Me to Be

Pondering that it is easy to know in my heart and mind, that God has a specific purpose for me. But not allowing myself to get caught up in a mental competition with others, over how He has used them, or blessed them, or given them seemingly more of an influence...that can be a definite trap at times. So i am thinking it is SO important that each of us know that He created us with a plan and a purpose, that He made uniquely for each of us! Maybe none of you struggle with this, but i am guessing we all do at times. So here is to a day of being glad that the Lord made us who we are. To be grateful for those around us who we love and care for and who love and care for us. To see the blessing in all the little distinct characteristics He has blessed us with!

Thinking that at those times when i may not understand God's ways and His timing, He is still working, and His ways are still best!! True wisdom will never come from my own plans and ideas, but from seeking the Lord and His ways and desires.

God Has a Plan

Thinking this morning about the fact that the Lord has a plan tailored for each of us! As i reflect on the years behind me, i see many different things...challenges, very hard times, good times, and wonderful blessings, and all the seemingly, inconsequential things in between. It reminds me that the Lord knows i need them all to refine me and make me what He wants me to be. It is my goal that i always be pliable in His hands that He will always be reflected in my life.

His Time and His Ways

Seems lately that i have lacked energy and have lost a bit of motivation. I am so thankful that the Lord is my strength, and that He enables me to do what it is He desires of me. He will also be my motivation when i listen to Him and ask for His direction. It doesn't always happen in my time frame, but always in the best time frame! I know that to be so because He sees it all! And He does what is best for those who love Him!

It's All About Him! Not Me

I am so thankful that God compares us to sheep in the 23rd Psalm! Sheep are known to be stubborn and stupid...so why am i glad for that comparison? Because it reminds me that what God says to me is not about my abilities or wisdom, but it is because of HIS love and mercy!! Psalm 23:1-3a--"The LORD is my shepherd; I shall not want [lack]. He makes me lie down in green pastures: He leads me beside the still waters. He restores my soul:" He protects, and provides, and restores (rejuvenates) my soul!! I am just so thankful for His love!! And i hope that like this encouraged me, it will also encourage others of you that are feeling weary or worn. I know we don't always share those things. But God knows our hearts. So, i pray this will help those who need it, like the Holy Spirit knew i did this morning.

Learning God's Ways Are Better

As i read God's Word, i am reminded that there are times when God gives people what they want, not because it is best for them, but so that they can come to a better understanding that it is not best for them. He didn't want it in the first place, but they insist, so He gives it...Sometimes, just like with them, it is the only way we learn...

God's Purpose Is Always Good

I am so thankful that though i may not understand all the reasons for the circumstances of this life, it does not mean God does not have a purpose. In fact, the contrary is true. God always has a good reason for all the events of my life! Never is He random or thoughtless! But He definitely has a much greater view than i do! My "sight" is limited. And just because i cannot see what He is doing ahead of time, does not mean He is not working. Oh, that i would trust and rest in Him more. He is always good and loving! I can always trust His heart. And His ability has no limits!!

God's Perfect 'Puzzle Piecing'

Thinking about how i love how God puts things together! Between last night's sermon and what/where i am studying in my quiet time, they fit together like puzzle pieces. It is so important that i be content doing whatever the Lord calls me to do. Also, to do it as unto Him--willingly, joyfully because i love Him, and with all my might! He is worthy of my best! And though i do not serve Him to get reward, He does bless obedience!

God's Ways Are Amazing

Thinking about how i can get sort of stuck in how I expect or presume God is going to do something. Then, when it doesn't happen that way, I get frustrated. But the truth is that God's ways and plans are so much more extraordinary than mine! And it causes me to realize that i need to just start opening my heart and mind, to pay attention to however He does things. Because however that is, it will be amazing and point people to His glory and ability!!

God Does Not Always Use Those That We Would Think

"For you see your calling brethren, how that not many wise men after the flesh, not many mighty, not many noble are called: But God hath chosen the foolish things of the world to confound the wise; and God hath chosen the weak things of the world to confound the things which are mighty:...That no flesh should glory in his [own] presence....That, according as it is written, he that glories, let him glory in the Lord." 1Cor. 1:26,27,29,31 Thinking that these verses pretty much cover what is on my mind this morning.

The Lord's Leading

I am thinking this morning that if i want the Lord to guide me in my days, then I need to stop and read His Word to know His ways. I also need to ask Him to impress on my heart what He wants me to do. I cannot expect Him to lead if i will not listen.

I love the fact that the Lord has a purpose for me and loves me! That it is not based on who i am, but because of who He is! And that He can use the "ordinary" person any way He chooses!

God's Timing

So, my husband goes to get the car inspected and starts texting me all the things that the mechanic says are wrong with it and have to be fixed. Honestly, it was causing me to become a little frustrated. BUT then, i go to read my email and the verse for the day is Romans 5:3 which says in the NLT, "We can rejoice too, when we run into problems and trials, for we know that they help us develop endurance." No mistake in His timing!

Wisdom

True Wisdom Comes from God

Thinking this morning that the wisdom of this world does not line up with the true wisdom of God! The "wisdom" of this world will change with the fickleness of mankind. But God's ways are constant, true, and reliable, always!! Searching His Word, and His ways, and living by them--that is where wisdom lies!

True Wisdom

Thoughts this morning...that wisdom is nothing to be claimed on my own. True wisdom comes from the Lord. He says, whoever asks Him for it, will receive it (James 1:5). He doesn't tell me to do this or that or to get it from someone else. Wisdom comes from knowing Him and His truths and allowing the Spirit to have total control in changing my life as a result. That also requires surrender on my part. Sometimes giving up my ways for His. But all the glory goes to Him for any true wisdom that any of us possess.

Wisdom and Other Things of Lasting Value

As i am reading in Proverbs, i am finding that when i think of Solomon being the one who "penned" it, it takes on a bit more meaning. He speaks a lot about seeking wisdom and making right choices. But he never tells us to seek the riches of this world. He was an extremely wealthy man!! But in the middle of all of it, he still realized what was most important--knowing truth, and being wise, accepting instruction, and understanding. In fact, he says to "buy" these things...makes me realize that it is in these things that one finds lasting and true value. Knowing God's Word and His truth! Living in such a way that His love for me is seen in the way that i love others. Obedience to His will (which at times is contrary to my own) and being there for those He has placed in my life. And as i ponder these things, i find that the things that God says are of real value are nothing that we can actually purchase with our currency. But they do come at a price:

the price of time and effort,

the price of being still long enough for the Spirit to speak to us,

the price of being courageous enough to obey even when it can be scary,

and the price of taking time to be there for others....

Different Forms of Wisdom

Pondering this morning that it is easy to think of wisdom as knowledge. But sometimes wisdom is not always about words. Sometimes it means i listen, or have compassion, or am just there for someone. And sometimes it means that i backup my words by living for the Lord so that others can see Him and not me. Sometimes the Lord wants me to speak, but always He wants me to love Him and live for Him. And always He wants me to love others. True wisdom will lift up the Lord and not myself...

Wisdom Is...

Wisdom is better than riches. Wisdom is that knowledge of God that then leads my life to reflect Him, and not myself. The Bible says that it is greater than riches, and i would agree! There is nothing like focusing on walking in a way that pleases Him!

Wisdom Is Greater Than Riches

Thinking about Solomon this morning and his incredible wealth and wisdom. And it occurs to me that God may not have blessed him with such wealth, if he had not asked for wisdom...hmmm...thinking that wisdom is the important part. When i have wisdom that comes from God, then it is of little consequence as to whether i am wealthy in material things or not. Because i understand that to know God's truths and to act accordingly is worth much, much more!

Asking for God's Wisdom

I am one who ponders things. If you have ever read what i write, you know that. But as i read God's Word and see how He tells us to ask Him for wisdom, it makes me wonder if sometimes i ponder, or over think, or try to solve a little too much on my own. Probably sometimes yes i do and sometimes no. But the truth is that i always need to be asking for God's wisdom first and foremost! His wisdom and ways so far exceed my own! And He even promises to give it generously and without scolding us for asking! So here is to starting off the day asking for God's wisdom and watching where He leads and guides. It is not enough to ask if i am not going to pay attention.

Always Seeking God's Wisdom

Thinking this morning about how easy it is to go about my day just assuming i know the right choices and decisions to make. But it is so important to ask the Lord for wisdom on a daily basis. Sometimes things may seem like the right choice, when God has something completely different in mind. So, as i start this Thursday, i am focusing on seeking His direction, listening to, and obeying His leading, no matter how big or small.

Godly Wisdom

Thinking this morning that wisdom comes not only from asking the Lord for it and following His ways. It also comes by trusting and resting in Him. It is not about my own personal thoughts or what i can "figure out." But simply resting and trusting in Him!

Help

Abundantly Available

"God is our refuge and strength, a very present help [abundantly available] in trouble. Therefore will not we fear, though the earth be removed, and though the mountains be carried into the midst of the sea; though the waters thereof roar, and be troubled, though the mountains shake with the swelling thereof. Selah."
Psalm 46:1-3

I love how the Lord uses His Word to touch my life right where i am! And how He uses what He used before to encourage me yet again–just in a different way. About 8 years ago now (presently 2013), the Lord used this scripture to get me through a very, very tough time in our family's life. My husband, David, was in a very serious car accident and was in the hospital for the next 6 weeks. Our "personal world" had completely flipped upside down. But the Holy Spirit, almost daily, reminded me of the phrase of God being "abundantly available." It pulled me through many long days! But today, as i was reading through this portion of scripture, looking for encouragement (in a completely different situation, but something that is a very large burden on my heart), i kept reading...and noticed how the scripture talks about basically the earth collapsing around us and still *choosing not to fear because...*God is our refuge and strength and abundantly available in trouble! When that car accident happened, there were many things that my husband had to recover from. His body had a lot of healing that had to take place. We spent many long hours at the hospital and many hours in prayer. Trusting and resting in the Lord did not make everything all of a sudden go away. But it did enable me to be able to get through it with His strength (because *His* strength never fails). So, it is not so much about making things go away but maybe more about seeing how the Lord gets us through them. I also noticed the little word at the end of these verses "Selah" which means to stop and ponder these things...so i took that time, and i realize that if i truly believe that God is my refuge and strength, and abundantly available in trouble, then i *won't fear*, but will rest in His strength and not my own solutions or ideas. I don't know where you are in your life–if all seems pretty good or if it feels like your world is falling apart–but take heart my friend and may you have a day filled with the strength and refuge that is found only in the Lord Jesus Christ!!

My Help Comes from the Lord, Maker of Heaven and Earth

This is a phrase in a song that comes from Psalm 124:8. As i read this, this morning, i thought about the first part of the verse, but then realized the last part that talks about God making the heavens and the earth really did add emphasis! To stop and ponder the heavens...i can't even begin to comprehend the expanse of it all! Yet God simply spoke it into existence! Then, to think of ALL that is in and on this earth...from the plains of Africa, to the depths of the ocean, to the highest mountain peak, to the layers of ice in the Antarctic, to the tiniest bacteria in a pond no one even knows about, to the jungles and all that lives in them, to the creatures that live far underground!! All of it, God knows all about because He created it all! This One, the God of the universe!! He, He is the One who helps me! He did all this and didn't even break a sweat! Why in the world would i not trust Him to be able to help me?!

My Help Comes from God

I love that i can be secure in the Lord!!! Nothing like it! The Creator God takes the time and cares enough to help me! Do i really understand how spectacular that is?! That He doesn't just ignore me or tell me He is too busy for me? But He chooses to love me and help me! It really is something worth taking the time to ponder!

"I will lift my eyes unto the hills, from where my help comes from. My help comes from the Lord, maker of heaven and earth."
Psalm 121:1-2

Who Am I Counting on to Win My Battles?

As i was reading in Psalm 108 this morning, it was talking about how vain it is for man to try to defeat his enemy. But with God we will do valiantly, and the enemy will be defeated. i don't know about you, but once in a while i can get caught up in thinking, well, if i am determined enough, or have the right attitude, or get some friends to encourage me...then i will be able to get through________. But that is not where the secret to defeating our enemies is (and the enemy is not always necessarily people). The victory comes when i give whatever it is to the Lord, and i let Him handle it!! Besides that, i will find peace and contentment in Him, rather than the stress and worry that comes when i try to fix things or overcome things on my own. So, i am determining to put my cares and concerns in His hands, for Him to do with as He sees best.

God's Faithfulness

I am so thankful that the Lord is loyal to me as His child! He is not obligated to be. And there is obviously no one who can force Him. But He loves me and chooses to be faithful no matter what! It also is inspiration for me to be loyal in return!

Thinking that it is more important that i ask the Lord to help me deal with each day with His attitude and looking through the eyes of His truth, rather than to always be asking for Him to change my circumstances.

Hope

Sweeter

I remember years ago when my mom used to talk about how she looked forward to Heaven (and she still does)...but back then i was younger and was not quite as ready as she was. I am older now and understand a little better that feeling. The older i get, and the better i get to know my Lord, His presence and the time we spend together continues to get sweeter. He is my Lord and Savior, but He is also my dearest friend! And the thought of being forever with Him is like nothing else!!

But, as i write this, i also definitely understand that our relationship getting sweeter is not because life is always easy or because i am always obedient (It is *not* His responsibility to make me "happy" all the time. If i had a "friend" who only ever told me what i wanted to hear, rather than being honest with me, they would *not* be a true friend.). Like anything that grows, it takes stretching, Son-shine, and nourishment. But as those things come about, i come to understand that they are good and bring about the best results. So, my perspective of *growing pains* changes to growing opportunities. I was with a group many years ago, that stressed that "attitude is everything"...and because our attitude greatly affects our perspective, it really does make a difference!! As each day passes, i want my life with the Lord to grow sweeter and sweeter! That would be my wish and prayer for you as well!

"Sweeter as the years go by, Sweeter as the years go by, Richer, fuller, deeper, Jesus' love is sweeter, Sweeter as the years go by. "

Hope

As i think of hope, i think of the fact, that for me, it brings two different ideas to mind. It brings the thought of r-e-a-l-l-y hoping something will happen, but not really sure it will. That is not a very confident hope, but an "I wish this would happen" sort of hope. Then, there is the hope that i place in the Lord! That is a whole different kind of thing. Because as i hope in the Lord, i can be sure that He will be true to His word!! It comes with confidence and sure expectation! It may involve waiting but waiting that is worth the while. There seem to be so many things that can cause me to worry or fret. But the truth is that God is still God, and He is still in control! There is no one who is beyond His grasp or reach. There is *nothing* that happens under the radar that He misses or didn't quite catch. As was brought to my attention in the last couple of days, political issues can make us panic when we see the condition of things in this world. But i must be careful that i not do that! I can trust God's heart completely! And when i do that, then i will trust Him with all the other things that are going on around me. He did not say, I will provide your needs as long as the government is doing what they should be. No, He simply promises to meet the needs of His children. He knew everything that was going to happen, and He still made the promise. He said He would never leave us or forsake us, and that was unconditional as well. All His promises are true!! He loves us sooooooo much!! And my hope must be in the One who loves me perfectly and is able to do abundantly above all that we ask or think! That is the hope that will get me through any day!! Confidence in Him who loves me most!!

Hope Requires Waiting

I am thinking this morning about hope. Thinking that when you do away with the idea of expectancy, then it is no longer hope. But on the practical side of that, how often do i get discouraged about how slow i think the Lord is in doing something--answering my prayers? And yet if He did things my way and in my time, what kinds of things would i miss? Because as i look back over my own history, He has rarely done things as i expected or in the time frame i would have maybe desired. But He has done them in ways that could only have been Him! Ways that bring Him glory and not me. In timing that is almost unbelievable! And the lessons i would not have learned near as well, as i waited along the way. God is beyond containment, and His ways beyond my imagination! That is a good thing!! My hope is in the Lord, who gives good things to His children (Matthew 7:11). After all He is our Heavenly Father and if we know how to give good things to our children, how Much More does He know how and is fully able!! Here's to a day full of looking to see what the Lord is doing through the process!

Hoping in God

Thinking this morning that the things, and circumstances, and people, in this world, are going to disappoint us, somewhere along the way. But God's Word will never change, and His truth gives us hope!! If i find myself discouraged, i am probably hoping in the wrong person/things. So, i am going to set my sights on purpose, today, to putting my hope and trust in God and His truths!!

True Hope Is in God's Word

As I think about the verse below, it comes to mind that to hope in something means that that is where i am putting my confidence. What i notice is that the writer does NOT say that he hopes in his friends, or his job, or his own efforts (i.e. what he can do for himself), or in what he hopes God is going to do for him. He is not hoping in pleasures, or excitement, or distractions. He is hoping in the truths of God's Word! Our culture does not really understand that because of the self-focus we are so naturally prone to. But there is nothing like focusing on who God is, and His ways, and His truths!! Those have never changed and will always be reliable!! The other things i mentioned earlier are at best temporary. But the truths of God's Word will go on for always!! That is where true hope is and the right place to put my hope and confidence!

"I hope in Thy word."
Psalm 119:147b

Scripture

The Beauty of Scripture

I love quiet mornings when i have no little ones at my feet, and there is no one else in the house. Don't get me wrong! I love the little ones i watch, and that my husband and son are around at times...but to have quiet, quiet time with my Lord is like nothing else! It gives me a chance to pray and read without distraction! This morning i was reading about people who made poor choices and was challenged to self-examine myself to see where it is i tend to do that and what excuses i use. Intriguing how i do that–like praying about something or for someone and then turning around and worrying about it/them, rather than trusting my God who is able to take care of it all! Or not doing something because i just don't feel like it. Knowing the right thing and not doing it is also sin. I am so glad the Lord always uses His Word to direct/redirect our lives! It may not be that you read scripture that applies in a way that you might *want* it to (for whatever you are going through), but if not, it will always be something you get a chance to use/will need to use later on down the road.

As i look back over the 48 years of my life (it's 2012), i think of the many scripture memory programs i was involved in, and the times i have spent in God's Word, and i am so very thankful for how the Lord brings His Word back to my mind when i need it! Just this morning, i was able to share scripture with someone who was having a tough morning. The Lord brought a specific scripture to my mind that was so appropriate for the situation! We are to encourage others (and ourselves) with scripture! But first we have to know it to be able to use it. Today, i am just so very thankful that i live somewhere where i am able to read scripture freely and in my own language! What a blessing!!

Loving the Flavors of God's Word

This morning, while i was sitting eating my English muffin and blackberry jam, i was thinking about how i enjoy all the flavors--the muffin, the butter, and the jam. And it made me mindful that that is how i should think of God and His Word...i should love it and enjoy all the "flavors" that it has! I should savor it like i do a good meal! After all, it is my sustenance in this life! God gives me exactly what i need. And when i see it that way, then i realize how sweet it is to the palate and good for me too!!

The Treasure of God's Word

I read a verse this morning about God's Word being a treasure! And as i thought about that, it came to mind how much i love my husband. And if he wrote a book that was all about him, and his ways, and his life, and the things he wanted me to know, i would read it, and love it, and it would definitely be a treasure to me! So why wouldn't it stand to reason that i would love God's Word like that?! He inspired it! and it is all about Him! and His ways! and the things He wants to be sure i know! He loves me sooo much more than my husband, David, loves me, or i love David. And i love Him more than i do my wonderful hubby. So, why would it be anything less than a treasure to me!! Thanking the Lord this morning for the treasure of His Word!

So Much in Scripture!

Thinking about how much the Lord puts in His Word:

truth	correction	redirection
hope	instruction	blessing

refuge

comfort

guidance

love

peace

Himself

forgiveness

wonder

joy

reconciliation

He gives us so much that will never fade away!! I am so blessed to live where i have the scriptures in my own language and the freedom to read it as often and as long as i want!! Its value is beyond measure!

Obedience

Whose Idea of Greatness?

I am thinking this morning about the fact that God's concept of what defines greatness, is very different than how the world defines it. In fact, the world would not even think they were talking about the same thing at all.

The world says you need to be most concerned about yourself and do whatever it takes to make a name for yourself, regardless of the "cost." After all one must make themselves happy, first and foremost. Also, to be great, you need to do important things to get *noticed*. But the ultimate goal is all about you.

God says if you want to be great, then you need to serve and minister to others. You need to love the Lord first and foremost! And to love others like yourself! Putting them first! It is so very contrary to what the world would like us to believe! God doesn't ask for perfection, but for obedience. He doesn't expect us to bring about the best results because that is His job!

So i am thinking there is a choice that i must make on a daily basis (sometimes even more often than that). Whose definition of greatness will i decide to accomplish? Or follow? It is a choice. Neither one will just happen. They both require work. So where will my efforts go?

Quick to Listen

As i read the scripture below, i think, well, yes, of course. But then i think about the natural tendency i have to talk. And i might even make excuses that God made me that way, after all. Some people are shy, and some people are not. But then the Lord brings to mind that this affects me more than just in conversations with other people. Being chatty is part of who i am. But there will always be refining that needs to take place in my life, as long as i am here on this earth. And if i use my love to talk as an excuse, then that is proof that i am *not* responding to the Lord on a daily basis like i should. If i don't listen well to those that i can see, how well will i listen to the Lord, who i cannot see in a physical form? The problem with not listening, is that then one tends to fill in the gaps of what they missed. And often we *don't* do that in the way that the other person intended things to be understood, and that can lead to wrong feelings/ misunderstanding...and yes even anger. And that *does* happen! We often hear what we think we will hear and not what is actually being said (My kids could probably tell some stories on me). I learned quite a few years back, that listening takes a conscious effort. I must put other things aside and focus on who is talking. What if God listened to me like i listen to Him or to others? I am so glad He is better than i! Swift to hear! Am i doing that? Or am i swifter to jumping to conclusions or filling in the gaps just however? In my spiritual life, i must be swift to hear the Lord! Not to hear what i want Him to say or make up my own reasoning without going to His Word! It means i must put other things aside and focus and listen! To ponder His words. To really take in what He knows i need at that point in time. And it also means when i do that, it will be much more natural to be a better listener to those around me. And if there is something important that the Lord wants me to share with someone else, He will still bring it to mind when it is then time for me to talk. There are many things that can distract us from listening, but it is my prayer today, that both you and i will listen more intently to the Lord and also to those who He brings "across our paths."

"Wherefore, my beloved brethren, let every man be swift to hear, slow to speak, slow to wrath [anger]: for the wrath of man worketh not the righteousness of God."
James 1:19-20

God's Ways Vs. Man's Ways

So i am thinking this morning about a subject that most of us women bristle at...don't stop reading, please. Submission is a topic that most people don't approach these days. But the truth of the matter is, that God gave each of us *specific roles.* It does not mean we are inferior, but it does mean that we have different things God wants us to accomplish. He made the man to rule over his household and the woman to care for the household and be the nurturer. Have you ever worked under 2 bosses? My husband used to be a vendor and he had a company boss and a store boss, in every store he serviced. It was not always an easy job to please them all. Have we ever thought about the fact that the Lord is just trying to save us from grief? But i also know that the curse of sin brought with it a desire in women to want to rule over their husbands (Genesis 3:15). And most of us would attest to the fact that we like to be in charge. Well, guess what...God says we don't get to do that with our husbands (Ephesians 5:22-28). But we argue that "You just don't understand my situation." But i am thinking about the fact that this is not an argument with my husband (our husbands) this is an argument with God and His ways. The culture, in which we live, says we have rights. We need to be happy, we need________ (you can fill in the blank). But what a different place this would be if the husbands would cherish their wives and the wives would respect and submit to their husbands! The world wants you to believe differently. Yet what i know to be true, is that God's ways are best! With obedience to Him, comes peace and contentment. I didn't say it would be easy–and we ladies feel the need to use our daily amount of words, sometimes at our husbands' expense–but obedience to the Lord is always well worth it! Why not use those daily words to encourage our husbands!! If we women would respect and honor our husbands (yes that includes submission), we would find that they, in turn, would be much more loving and caring.

He Already Knew

Ever had one of those days or maybe a few of them, when you know the Lord has led you to do something, but you were thinking it would have a different result than what you are seeing? I have to remind myself that He already knew how things would go and what effect it would have. But He still asked me to be obedient to His call. So, it comes down to that *trusting issue again.* Who am i trusting? Am i obedient out of love for my Lord or because i expect something specific? I am called to be obedient, therefore along the way, i must also resign myself to trust the Lord to take my actions and bring about the effect He wants. So, i am deciding here and now, to do my best to surrender the results to the Lord (that means no worrying or anxiety) because Romans 8:28 is still true today for those who love the Lord! He makes promises to His children, and He always keeps them!! My responsibility is to obey...and to trust Him with the rest!!

Obedience–Not a Bad Word

Oh, the excuses i can make, at least in my mind, about why i would rather not do something. Will it really do any good or make a difference to anyone else? But then, i am reminded that i am commanded to obey what the Lord wants me to do. He does not say that i must understand it or grasp why, first. I need to trust His will and leading more than my own!! After all, He is the Creator, not me! As i read in the book of Judges, in my Bible, this morning, i saw how God gave very specific commandments to His people Israel, and they chose to disobey (and it is a choice). And it says that the generations to come did not know the things that the Lord had done for Israel, and they did evil in the sight of God. Sin has much farther-reaching effects than i think about at times. And it only takes one deliberate act of disobedience to get the ball started, so to speak. When i choose to disobey because of my lack of knowledge or whatever excuse i make, it creates distance between me and the Lord, which then makes for a better breeding ground for selfishness. And when i think of that, i think of how selfishness is with sin, like a pond is for bacteria– a perfect place for growth. The truth is, though, that when i obey the Lord and leave everything else to Him, there is peace and contentment. For me, the part i have to work on most, is leaving the results to Him. On the flip side however, we never can tell how far our obedience can go to encourage and inspire others. I have no idea who will or will not read this, and i want the Lord to use it to touch lives. But the truth is that i know the Lord wants me to write it. So, i will choose to obey and to trust Him with whatever He wants to do with it. Whoever you are, i pray that the Lord will give you a heart to obey His leading and the courage to follow through!

Not Giving into Sin

Thinking on how it takes a conscious effort to decide, ahead of time, that we will refuse to give into sin! Besides that, God needs to be first in my life, and if that is so, then i will want to please Him and not sin against Him! My food for thought for the day…

My Responsibilities?

Thinking about the fact that there are certain things that God has called me to do-- without a doubt. But that does not mean that every opportunity or problem to be solved is my duty to accomplish. I am pondering the fact that often i give an answer to someone before consulting the Lord. Instead, what i should do is to take the time to consult the One, to whom i belong, before saying yes or no.

Yielded to the Holy Spirit's Working in Me?

I have been reading about Saul and his jealousy toward David, as well as the many things he tried to do to get rid of David. And several things come to mind. The first being, that no matter what someone else's actions are toward me, i am still accountable for me. My actions are not excused because of theirs. Repeatedly scripture tells of how Saul did something, and yet David behaved himself wisely. The second thing that comes to mind is that comparing myself to someone else is never profitable! It either leads to discontentment or to pride. Neither of them are pleasing to the Lord. As i sit pondering these things, i realize that they are much easier said than done. But i also know that, as a Christian, i am indwelled by the Holy Spirit! And God promises to give His children all they need to live a godly life! So, it is not a question of whether i, personally, am able to accomplish this. It is actually more about being yielded to His Spirit and watching what He can do in and through me. Just wanting to be sensitive to the Holy Spirit's voice and leading in my life...which at times means changing how or what i may be doing...

Obedience to God

Thinking this morning on obedience...God asked people in Bible times to do things that they thought of as dangerous or definitely not their first choice...kind of like today. But the truth is, just as i was expected to obey my parents, and the same was expected of our kids (with David and me), so i/we are expected to obey our Heavenly Father! Sometimes we don't understand or really just don't want to. But above all others, He is most worthy of my honoring Him with obedience! That's just what is right! Besides that, it shows Him my love, and reverence for Him as well.

Pliable in God's Refining Process

Pondering this morning...God's refining process in my life...He calls me to obey Him fully and wholeheartedly! Yet He knows humanity and that we do not always do as we should, and He gives second chances...don't get me wrong. We are not to be complacent or purposely disobedient. But God is always gracious, always merciful, and always loving! All that said i want to be pliable and more obedient with every day that He gives me...

Total Obedience Means No Questions Asked

As i continue to read through the book of Joshua, there are so many battles. And i must admit, i don't always understand God's ways. But as i look at the accounts, what i do see, is Joshua in total obedience to God, no questions asked!! Wow! It definitely challenges me to obey the Lord my God, no questions asked!! Quite a challenge when the rubber meets the road...

Obedience to God is not always easy or my natural instinct, but always right and always worth the effort!!

Obedient in Spite of the Struggles

Pondering this morning that life can be a struggle at times...for all kinds of reasons. But i am to remain obedient to the Lord, enduring and self-disciplined. In that, He will be my strength and my peace! It is when we realize that we have no strength or answers of our own, that we are more likely to call out to Him and look to Him. He wants to make Himself known to us and to those around us. So, if that is what it takes, then that is what He will do. It's not a bad thing...in fact it is wonderful that He loves us so much!!

Obedience

As i read through Jeremiah, i am reminded that the Lord calls me to obedience, no matter what the results are. At times, i must confess that i want to both obey, AND make things happen. And when it doesn't happen that way, i get discouraged. But i am only responsible to obey my Lord. Trusting and resting in whatever He sees best to bring about. He loves me, and i can always trust His heart to be good! Willingness and obedience are both my responsibility to the Lord! But the results are His to take care of! Besides that, i can never even come close to accomplishing what He can!!

Listening to Him and Not Me

As i sit pondering God's Word this morning, He impresses on me that instead of always trying to figure things out, i need to be more aware of His still small voice. He wants me to be obedient and sensitive to what He wants, moment by moment. Honestly, i find this to be a bit of a challenge for me at times. Only by His strength and grace, does that happen! So, here's to facing the challenge! With Him all things are possible!!

Diligence in Obedience

As i have been reading in Jeremiah, on a daily basis, lately, i am impressed with his obedience, even when there seems to be no results. He is diligent in his work! As i ponder that, the Holy Spirit impresses on me that the love that Jeremiah must have had for the Lord, AND for the people he was trying to get to listen, must have been amazing! And i am challenged to love the Lord more and also those He has placed in my life! To love them and pray for them. Possibly help guide or encourage them, as He leads me. But not for my glory or praise, but because i love the Lord and i love them!

His Faithfulness

Still...

No matter what comes my way in this life, God's faithful love remains constant!! His mercies are still new every morning! His grace is still sufficient! I can still cast all my cares on Him, and He still cares for me! He is still my strong tower/ refuge/fortress! I am still safe in His care! He still hears me when i call Him! His strength is still made perfect in my weakness! He is still abundantly available! He is still the loving Savior who went to Calvary to pay the price for my sins! HE IS STILL WHO HE HAS ALWAYS BEEN!! LOVING, CARING, AND PROTECTING HIS OWN!! NOTHING WILL EVER CHANGE THAT!! There IS something to smile about!

"For I am persuaded, that neither death, nor life, nor angels, nor principalities, nor powers, nor things present, nor things to come, nor height, nor depth, nor any other creature, shall be able to separate us from the love of God, which is in Christ Jesus our Lord."
Romans 8:38-39

Repetition

I am thinking back this morning to the days of homeschooling my kids...repetition was a very good teacher. It had a way of embedding an idea or concept into their minds. It was my goal that they learn and not just check a box. And though i am not always fond of repeating things, i am so very thankful that the Lord loves me enough to be patient with me, until my slow minded self picks up on something. Often i get caught up in the fact that i am the one having to go through things again and again, but... the "teacher" has to repeat those things as well...hmm...thank you Lord for loving me enough to take the time to make me more like You!

God's Reliability

I am so thankful that God is completely reliable! Nothing catches Him off guard or by surprise! He is faithful and over all!! I can rest in Him without worry!! And there is amazing security there! Beyond explanation or our own understanding!

What if God Reacted/ Responded Like We Do?

Studying this morning about how we can get caught up in doing things for the praise of man. Consequently, i am thinking we all can get wrapped up in this. So, when people don't praise, or thank, or notice us, we get discouraged, and sometimes even want to throw up our hands and say, "I quit." But then, it hit me...what if God did that every time we were less grateful or appreciative than we should be? So glad His actions and responses are based on His unchanging ways and His never-ending love!! But it does inspire me to be much more thankful on a more moment by moment basis for all that He does, all the time!!!! It is definitely not because any of us are deserving, but because He is an amazing God, all the time!!

God is My Best Source for All Things!

Walking away from my quiet time this morning, i am thinking about how amazing it is to have loving friends and family in my life! People who will encourage me, and challenge me, laugh with me, and cry with me! Those who are lots of fun and those who are a bit more serious. Those i can vent to and those who will give me godly, honest responses. They are all a part of my life for good reason. But the truth of the matter is-- that they are not all that i need. I need to remember that it is the Lord who i need to go to for truly solving problems. Why? My friends aren't good enough? Not at all! But God...God is all knowing, God is all forgiving, He is Almighty God! He is always available! Not only does He always have the perfect answer, but He is also able to make it happen! He is never caught off guard or has a bad day. He is faithful, loving, and true, no matter what! He can convict me and change my heart's desires and attitudes. He knows exactly where to redirect my ways when i am walking in a direction i should not be going in. I am so very grateful that He is my Savior and Lord! He is my Heavenly Father!! And He is the very best friend i could ever have!! I am not saying it is a bad thing to talk to your friends or to go to them when you have a need. But they will never be able to help you like God can help you. They can help you with the things they can see, at times. And they can listen to what you share with them. But often the things we cannot see are the most harmful...Thinking that it is so important that i ask the Lord to guard my heart! Because everything else is affected by it. I want to be always mindful that my best help will always come from the Lord!!

Lifetime of Construction--But Not Excuses

Thinking this morning that the Lord has a way of making sure i am listening to Him. Both in my quiet time and in my ladies' Bible study, i read about different kinds of construction...one was the temple, the other being the ark. But since i woke up this morning not so thrilled with what i saw in me, it was a good reminder that just like the ark and the temple had many facets of construction and took quite some time (years) to build, so the Lord is constructing this life of mine. I am so thankful that He does not just walk away from me and say, "Forget it, it's not worth the effort or the trouble!" But this Christian life is a process and as long as i am on this earth, He will be working in and constructing my life to be more like Him--whatever that may take. My job is to be firm in His ways and pliable in His hands...

Resting in God

I haven't really been on Facebook at great length lately, and as i am reading posts, happy and frustrated, and in all sorts of directions, i have two choices. I can get swept away in them, or i can breathe a sigh of relief that God is still God! and still in control! No matter what is going on and where. It doesn't mean i have no concern or anything like that. But it does mean that i can go to bed at night and rest in His care and know that He is the One who directs my life! I can sleep peacefully because i am not carrying burdens that are not meant for me to carry or be jealous because someone else seems to have things better. So, here's to resting where we should be--in the wonderful care of our Savior!! Sweet dreams my friends!

Thinking that God always takes care of His own! But He will convict us and work at redirecting us, possibly even punish us when we are in sin or going in a direction He knows is not best.

God Over ALL

Thinking that i need to really understand that God is God in this earth! With every care i pick up, whether big or small, i need to remind myself that He is God over that too! And on the flip side, He is God over the good things too! I need to be giving Him the glory and praise for them as well! Meditating on the scriptures...nothing quite like it!

Perfect Hearted, and God Over All!

Thinking this morning, that as i ponder the fact that God is God of both Heaven and earth, that how i act on what i believe, is so very important! Does it affect the way i act? It should! More importantly does it affect the way i think? Do i worry? Am i fearful? I know our first instinct would be to say that that is normal, but that is an excuse. My God is God over all!! And all that He does is for the good of His children because He loves us!! So where is my trust and rest, really?! In myself or in God?! It is BEST placed in God!!! My food for thought.

God Is True to Himself

As i sit this morning thinking about the fact that God is always true to His promises even when His children walk in rebellion, i am so grateful that He is always faithful! But i am also very aware that it is not an excuse to sin and have a complacent attitude. His true love for me creates a response of wanting to love Him, with all that i am!! This includes obedience...here's to a day of focusing on and worshipping Him!

God's Character

Thinking and praising God for the fact that His character has everything to do with Who He is and not on my undeserving, unworthy self! I need always to be mindful that i am a sinner saved by grace! All sin is worthy of death, and mine had to be paid for on that cross, just as much as anyone else's! So very thankful for His grace, and mercy, forgiveness, and love!!

Only God Can Change Hearts

Pondering this morning how long Jeremiah prophesied and continued to prophesy. All the while he acknowledged God and His unlimited ability. My thoughts are drawn to the fact that i can change events and circumstances around me. That's not a hard thing to do. But only God can change hearts! No matter how hard or complacent they may be, He can draw people to Himself! I can't do that...but i can keep praying and (when He leads) share His truths in love. Watching to see what He does!

God is Always Working

Thinking on the fact that just because I don't see what God is doing or what His time frame is, in no way means He is not true to His promises or working on behalf of His children. He IS faithful now and always will be! Not because we are deserving but because He loves us fully and lavishly!

Resting in God's Care

As i continue reading in 2 Kings about how God used Elisha and protected him as well, i am again reminded that God absolutely takes care of and protects His own!!! What a wonderful place to rest, when i honestly and truly lay my cares at His feet!

The New Year

Every new year holds something different for every person. It causes me to think that as believers, it is so important to take the time and reflect on the goodness of the One, who gives us life and breath, and the blessings we too often take for granted. He is the One who gets us through our years past and prepares the paths ahead of us in the years to come...

His Peace

Peace and Rest

Thinking that there is an indescribable peace when i really, truly put my trust in God for everything! But it will never come from what i see, or own, or do, or what kind of logic man can offer...this peace can ONLY come from God!! I am choosing to rest there.

Stillness Brings Rest

To be still and focus on the fact that God is God, is the most peaceful, content, and secure place to be!! So why is it that we – i - spend so much time "elsewhere?"

Food for thought...

"Be still and know that I am God:
I will be exalted among the heathen,
I will be exalted in the earth.
The LORD of hosts is with us;
the God of Jacob is our refuge. Selah"
Psalm 46:10-11

Thinking that the joy and peace that the Lord gives is something the world cannot replicate nor take away!

Praise the Lord!

Content and At Peace

Thinking this morning, as i was reading in my Bible, that i was struck with the fact that comparing only leads to trouble...and in certain ways that i know need work, i was working on contentment with who and where i am and what i am doing. But before dinner tonight i realized i was doing some other comparing (not necessarily with what the struggle usually is). But nevertheless comparing. And as i got on Facebook after supper, and read the poster right below this post on my page, i read "the fruit of the Spirit is peace." Sometimes i can get discouraged with not being where i need to be. BUT i am so very thankful that the Lord continues to work in my life to convict and refine me!! And when i do yield to the Spirit, He not only leads me and directs me, but He fills me with His peace! Hmmm, where would i rather be? Content and at peace or comparing and discontent? Pondering these thoughts this evening...

Listening to the Lord, Rather Than Myself

As i sit here this morning, i realize that often, it is listening to my own voice and my own thoughts, that brings anxiety, frustration, and disappointment. Trying to see things through the perspective of the world is no help either because then i have to be totally dependent on my own strength. But praise the Lord, the Holy Spirit takes me to the verse that says God gives peace that the world cannot give! With His peace, i don't need to be troubled or afraid! But in order to live without fear or letting things get to me, i have to listen to His voice rather than my own. And i have to follow His ways (which i learn in His Word) rather than my own... He offers peace! However, if i am so busy trying to solve things on my own, i will never know the sweetness of it...

His Power

Wimpy or Strong?

Those who know me know that i consider myself a bit wimpy. But as i was at ladies' Bible study last night, something was said that kind of made me stop and think. I am a child of God! And as such, i am indwelt by the Holy Spirit. The Holy Spirit is all powerful and unhindered! He indwells me! He empowers me! I am *not* a wimp! Because *i am a child of the* Almighty!

But when i start focusing on myself, then i get discouraged and disheartened. The devil will be glad. And i am tempted to become a bit stagnant in my daily life. That is definitely not what i want! My God is all powerful, and there is no contest between Him and anyone else! So, i need to claim His strength as my own and do whatever it is that He calls me to do, whenever He calls me!

It is not as though i didn't know these things before, but sometimes the things we know seem to come alive in a little brighter light! So i am going to be thankful that i can do all things through Christ who gives me strength!! Going into my day with that in mind!! And hoping this has encouraged you to do the same.

Where Does My Help Come From?

Walking away from my quiet time this morning, i am thinking about how amazing it is to have loving friends and family in my life! People who will encourage me, and challenge me, laugh with me, and cry with me! Those who are lots of fun and those who are a bit more serious. Those i can vent to and those who will give me godly, honest responses. They are all a part of my life for good reason. But the truth of the matter is-- that they are not all that i need. I need to remember that it is the Lord who i need to go to for truly solving problems. Why? My friends aren't good enough? Not at all! But God...God is all knowing, God is all forgiving, He is Almighty God! He is always available! Not only does He always have the perfect answer, but He is also able to make it happen! He is never caught off guard or has a bad day. He is faithful, loving, and true, no matter what! He can convict me and change my heart's desires and attitudes. He knows exactly where to redirect my ways when i am walking in a direction i should not be going in. I am so very grateful that He is my Savior and Lord! He is my Heavenly Father!! And He is the very best friend i could ever have!! I am not saying it is a bad thing to talk to your friends or to go to them when you have a need. But they will never be able to help you like God can help you. They can help you with the things they can see, at times. And they can listen to what you share with them. But often the things we cannot see are the most harmful...Thinking that it is so important that i ask the Lord to guard my heart! Because everything else is affected by it. I want to be always mindful that my best help will always come from the Lord!!

Problems

Some days i sit down to write, and i know roughly what it is the Lord wants me to share. But today is one of those times where He is going to do the sharing. Because i am not sure where He wants it to go today. I was reading in Psalms this morning, and David was talking about how he was taking his problems to the Lord. He needed help, and he knew God would give it to Him. He also made the statement that the enemies were too strong for him. I am so glad that there is nothing stronger than God!! I mean, i don't doubt that, but sometimes i think i need to state it *more often*. And though some may think it is just one of those pat responses, i am here to say, it is not like that at all. I have lived long enough and been through enough, to know the truth in it by experience. There are several people who come to my mind, who have been or are currently struggling with some things. They are people who are dear to me and have confided in me. And sometimes i can give them guidance, but not always. Sometimes i have to just offer my prayers. And while sometimes that makes me (and maybe them too) feel helpless, it shouldn't. God is the best solver, healer, deliverer, and confidant there is!! I believe He gives us each other to help us through our lives. He compares us to a body — all different parts, but all necessary to each other. But He must be the first one i go to for guidance and help! He is all sufficient and better than any earthly father! This morning i was challenged in a Bible study i am doing, to write out a timeline with things on it that did not seem so great at the time, but that as i look back i can see what God did! It was really good to remind myself of those times and the ways He made me more like Himself through that process! He does not give or allow hard times in our lives to be mean. Rather, He uses it as a refining process to help us to look more like Him and to bring glory to His name. i don't ever want to be bitter because of something that happens in my life. But i *do* want to learn, and to grow, and to seek to have the Lord's perspective through it all. I hope it is the same for you my friend. Trusting that the Lord will use this to minister to those who need ministering to.

So God Can Receive the Glory

As i sit, and read, and ponder on God's Word, i realize that it is easy to point our fingers at others and what they did wrong (Scripture is full of examples). But i also realize that if i (and maybe you too) were honest, we like things in life to be easy. In fact, maybe like me, you have come across those who seem to think that if things don't go smoothly, they must not be part of God's will. But then i think of the words of Paul in 1 Corinthians... "And He [the Lord] said unto me, My grace is sufficient for thee: for my strength is made perfect in weakness. Most gladly therefore will I [Paul] glory in my infirmities, that the power of Christ may rest upon me. Therefore I take pleasure in infirmities, in persecutions, in distresses for Christ's sake: for when I am weak, then am I strong." And it is very clear to me why the Lord allows trials or even places them in my life. We need to see His strength and give Him glory!! And also, so that i can know firsthand how He gets me through this life He has planned for me! To Him be all the glory and praise!

Far Reaching Power of God

Thinking this morning that there is soooo much that God does, all the time, all over the world… And i so wish i could grasp it! That i could visualize more than just where i am, and what is going on around me! To really understand how awesome He is!! Especially thinking about how He holds the Pacific Ocean in place and yet He holds all the oceans in place!! Amazing!!

God Is Greater

No matter what, God is Greater!! And i need to be praising Him accordingly! I need to stop stressing, or worrying, or over thinking things, or taking on things that are not my responsibility. I need to trust Almighty God, who is greater than any and every care i could have!! To Praise Him!! He is worthy of ALL praise!! And He will make His presence known!

What I Can't Handle, God Can

Thinking this morning that i used to say that God doesn't give me anything i can't handle, but that is not really true. The truth is, that at times He does give me things i cannot handle, so that His ability and strength can be seen instead of mine! I am also reminded that when those times do come, rather than complaining, I need to be quick to point myself and others to Him! What an opportunity to share Christ with others because of what He has done and is doing in difficult times!

God's Ability Trumps My Inability!

Thinking this morning that i can easily get caught up in my inability to do something or go through something. But God's ability always trumps my inability!! He is my strength!! He is the One who is truly able! When i try to do things in my own strength, it only leads to frustration and stress. And God doesn't get any glory from that.

God's Power -Beyond!

Pondering how often in this past week, the Lord has had me reading scripture that reminds me that His power is so far beyond our limits!! It surely does not fit in any box of our imagination!! I must guard myself from thinking, that because i don't understand the how, the why, or even to what extent, that He is not working. I am confident that He does so much that we just can't even fathom it!

Christmas

Christmas Spirit

(December 21, 2013)

So...i love Christmas, and Thanksgiving, and New Years! I enjoy shopping for gifts, and having company, and going to parties -- the whole bit. But there are some thoughts that keep coming to mind lately. Sometimes, as much as we *want* to be in the "holiday spirit," it can get a bit overwhelming. We all know that it is not always a pleasant experience to shop at this time of year or to deal with the extra traffic that is in most places. The very thing that we are trying to do to make it extra special, can become the problem. We are so busy doing this and buying that, that we don't have time to spend with those we love-- and all the time getting more tired. So that also becomes an obstacle. Now don't get me wrong, i will probably *always* like to buy presents and have special parties. But it does come to mind, that to be Christ-like, i need to be giving and thankful all year long. Then, maybe it wouldn't be so stressful to try and cram it all into a month or so, every year. While all the hustle and bustle is not necessarily wrong, it does not always lend itself to taking the time to be still and thinking on the gift of our Savior, or even on blessing others as an outpouring of God's love to us. I am not pointing fingers at anyone (except maybe myself). But there is much to be said for balance rather than extremes. I want to show my love to the Lord by showing it to others. But a heart of love so far exceeds just lots of gifts or exorbitant spending, any day. May your Christmas truly be filled with the love of our Lord and letting His love pour out of you, and towards others. You will be a blessing as well as be blessed.

MERRY CHRISTMAS!

Christmas Distractions

Contemplating that (though i really enjoy the festivities of this time of year) i should really take some extra time to ponder all that Christ's birth means in my life as a believer! Yes, we give because God gave His Son for us, and it started at His birth...but do i think about that when i give a gift? Or do i just get caught up in the shopping and the craziness that it sometimes entails? Just thinking that we all make extra effort to add things to our daily responsibilities and such. But this is not my birthday, this is His Birthday!! I should be going out of my way to bring Him glory and to think on what His birthday means. Don't get me wrong, i am not anti-tradition. But i do think--maybe not for you, but for me at times--that in honoring His birthday, we actually tend to get so busy that we push to the side that the holiday is about Him! I don't want to let it get to be that way with me this year. I want to focus on worshiping my Savior and really thinking on HIS birthday, rather than getting distracted by everything else.

His Parenting

Fear

"For ye have not received the spirit of bondage again unto fear; but ye have received the Spirit of adoption, whereby we cry, Abba, Father."
Romans 8:15

I am sure i have read that verse hundreds of times because Romans 8 is one of my favorite chapters in the Bible. But i have never really stopped and examined what it meant and the impact that it should have on me (and all believers). The first thing that jumps out at me, is that

f e a r is b o n d a g e.

And as an unbeliever, who has no hope in Christ or faith in what He does on a daily basis, it is obvious why one would be fearful. It makes perfect sense.

B U T as an adopted child of God, i have access to my Heavenly Daddy (that is what Abba means). A dad who is sooo much better than any earthly dad (Matthew 7:7-11)! A dad who will withhold no good thing from them who ask! One who loves us so much more than anyone else can ever even imagine!!! A dad who is in control of ALL THINGS! A daddy who has a plan for good, and not for evil, for *ALL* His children! And contrary to some peoples' opinions, there is none that can keep Him from doing what it is He is going to do (They simply miss out on the blessings along the way because they were uncooperative). So as i put this into the proper perspective, why in the world do i give way to fear??

I have a wonderful earthly daddy! I am blessed! And i know he would do anything he could for me! But my Heavenly Daddy is better than my earthly daddy can ever be!! Because He not only wants what is best for me, but He is always capable and always does what is best for me!! He is limitless, and His love for me is boundless!! I have direct access to Him because He is my dad!! I am trying to really get a grasp on the safety and security that comes in knowing who He really is and that i need to simply be still and watch Him do the amazing work that He does daily! To let go of whatever fear i am clinging to and to realize that, in God there is peace!!

God-the Perfect Father

Though our kids are grown now, and parenting takes on a little different perspective, David and i have been parents now for 26 years (in 2013). It has given us a *little* bit of experience. I think about the years of training & teaching (not sure it ever completely ends) and how we desired our kids to learn and to grow. Sometimes they learned the easy way, and sometimes they had to learn the hard way. But we never decided it was time to stop teaching because it was hard. And we knew that some things had to be struggled through. We tried to spare them as much pain as possible. But there is a reason for the term "growing pains." They are a part of life. But then my mind goes to my Heavenly Father– the perfect parent! He loves us perfectly! And because He wants what's best for us, He allows us, at times, to do our 'own thing'–so we then can see that His ways are better! He also, at times, allows pain so that we can understand His incomparable comfort! He will never let us go so far that He cannot bring us back. He *will* reign us back in! After all, He is also our Shepherd! He will allow us to be refined, seemingly by being in the fire, not to destroy us–that is *never* His goal!! But so that we will shine for Him and reflect His beauty! No one ever gets strong by sitting around. I do believe sometimes we (or at least i am tempted to) think that God is being harsh or cruel. Why wouldn't He make this easier? He could! But then i remember what Matthew 7:11 says, and it is true! "If ye then being evil, know how to give good gifts to your children, HOW MUCH MORE shall your Father which is in heaven give good things to them that ask Him." God is the perfect parent! He knows us completely, loves us unconditionally, and is in control over ALL things!! May we all rest there!!

Parenting

I was reading this morning in 1 Chronicles (many, many genealogies) and read about someone who had 150 kids! Wow! I must admit i am really glad that the Lord did not bless me with that many kids–it is a lot of responsibility! But i *am* a mom of 2 (though they are grown now). And while they were young, they were my (and my husband's) *total* responsibility. However, now that they are grown, there is a different role i play in their lives.

I remember many years ago when i graduated high school and went to be part of a Christian touring group. I had lived in Colorado and was moving to Florida. Big change!! My mom flew out there with me and left a few days later. But she wrote me a letter when she left, telling me she was thankful that the Lord had shared me with her, and now she was basically cutting the apron strings, and giving me *completely* to Him (Still makes me a bit emotional). And i realize that there comes a point when i, as a mom, am no longer responsible to the same extent that i used to be. So, what *is* my responsibility?

To pray without ceasing!

To be willing to help, *when the Lord wants me to,*

but also, to be quiet, *when He wants me to.*

I love being a mom and am so thankful for the children the Lord has blessed me with! But mothering is not always the same over the years. God's fathering, however, is always the same!! And i am so thankful that my 'kids' are safe and secure in their Heavenly Father's care!! He has always been the perfect parent and always will be!

Praise His name!!

God, the Better Parent

Pondering this morning, that when i start to worry about something, not only do i need to pray about it, but i need to remember that God is a Much Better parent than i am!! He loves me more and gives me more than i will ever love or give to my kids!! It is so important that i trust His heart and remember that He is a better parent than i will ever be or imagine to be!! Oh, to really be able to grasp that!

Belonging to Him

Thinking this morning about what it means to say God is my God...and among many things that came to mind and i journaled about, is that it is a huge thing that He is God of ALL, and yet...He loves me, and is concerned about every part of my day. Just average me, and yet i am His child and that makes me important to Him!! He is God, and He is pure hearted in all He does!! How blessed to belong to Him!

Understanding God's 'Parenting'

I seem to understand the Lord and how He deals with me, on a better level, because i have been a parent. When i used to give my kids instruction, it was always best if they heeded it the first time. If not, then there were consequences-some mild and some a little more drastic, depending on the situation. And when God gives me direction or instruction, and i obey or follow right away, then obviously that is best! But if i put it off, or ignore it completely, then just like there were consequences for my children, there are consequences for me, as God's child. How i long to be a better listener and to obey more quickly, as each day passes! And that i will know His peace and contentment because i am doing His will!

God Is in Every Part of My Life

Thinking that i am so thankful that God is in EVERY detail of my life. The big and little ones, and all the ones in between that don't seem to make much difference to us. It is all for His purpose in making me the person He wants me to be. After all, i belong to Him! He loves all His children so very much and is so very patient with us all! But if i abuse that, there will be punishment (as any responsible parent would give). So, as i start my day, and as the day progresses, i want to be mindful of His hands at work in my life...whatever that may look like, i can trust His heart!

Boundaries Are a Good Thing

I was thinking this morning about a study that was done, which shows that kids who grow up with consistent rules, guidelines, and punishment for disobedience, are actually much more content and secure than those who do not. And it made me think about how my Heavenly Father gives me guidelines and rules that He desires me to follow, and consequences when i do not. When i am in His Word and know Him and His ways, and am obedient to Him, then i am secure and at peace--content and even blessed. But to be able to do that, i must be in His Word! I am so thankful that i live in a place where i have His Word and it is in my own language! Another one of those blessings that i don't always think to be thankful for!

Precious in His Sight

What a wonderful thing to take the time to reflect on how much the Lord, my Heavenly Father, loves me! How precious all His children are to Him!! I am afraid that we spend too much time pondering the wrong things... and as a parent wouldn't i want my kids thinking, at least every so often, how much i love them! So why wouldn't God want the same!

"How precious also are Thy thoughts into me, O God! How great is the sum of them! If I should count them they are more in number than the sand: when I awake I am still with Thee."
Psalm 139:17-18

Salvation

The Gift of Salvation

Pondering God's grace and mercy in the sending of His Son. Thinking of the amazing love of Christ in His willingness to leave Heaven and come to this earth! Knowing it was for the ultimate reason of paying the price for our sins by dying on a cross! Not His sins but ours! That is love!!

Christ's Payment for Our Sin

Isaiah 53:5-" But He was wounded for our transgressions, He was bruised for our iniquities: the chastisement of our peace was upon Him; and with His stripes we are healed." I am thinking today of the price that Christ paid on my behalf and how horrific the price was! He gave and gives so much! Yet, how quick i can be to complain. Shame on me! I will never give as much as He gave...He was mortally wounded for the sins that i commit! That you commit! For those He suffered and died! Not for His own sin. He had none!! I used to think, as an ignorant child, that because He was God, it didn't actually hurt. How wrong i was! He was in a human body! It was excruciating pain!! Such love He has shown!

Easter Victory Before Earthly Worries

I am thinking this morning as i scroll through Facebook posts, that there are quite a few people struggling in numerous areas and ways. And it can become so easy to get caught up in our struggles (Don't get me wrong i am not minimizing the struggles or saying they are not real). And yet this is the week (the week before Easter), we think of Christ's sacrifice for and victory over our sin!! I don't want to be so distracted, that i miss the victory in Christ! The devil and/or my circumstances don't get to take away the joy that is the basis for my Christian faith and my life!! To God be the glory!

Sin Covered Completely!

As i look out at the snow on the ground this morning i think of how God reveals Himself to us through His creation. My mind goes to the fact, that the way the snow covers the ground completely, so my sins are covered (all of them) by the blood of Christ! None of them are left uncovered or unforgiven!! Praise the Lord!! How amazing!

Sin

All Sin, Seen and Unseen Has an Effect

Thinking that though others don't necessarily see what i would call the sins of the mind-- like worry, anger, stressing, bitterness, (whatever it might be)...they are still sins that need to be dealt with! They will eat us up from the inside out, usually. And they are not less sin because others may not see them. God sees my heart! So, i need to be aware of what He sees and how that is impacting my fellowship with Him.

Idols in Our Lives?

Pondering this morning about how easy it is to shake my head at how foolish the people of Israel were, at certain times in history. Today i was reading in Judges, about how many different gods they worshipped after a certain judge died. And it dumbfounds me, until i look at our own country, and even in our churches, at how easy it can be to let things and people become more consuming in my life than God. And i came up with quite a list of things that are not always bad, in and of themselves, but can become idols because they can consume us:

success	control	church
jobs	beauty	activities
freedoms/rights	strength	notoriety
pride	wealth	homes
projects	lack of wealth	possessions
good deeds	family	knowledge
our spouse	friends	fitness

And the list could go on. But as i thought of this, i realized that there are, at times, certain things or people i have a tendency to give more time and effort to, than i do to my Lord and Savior. So, lest i shake my head at others, i need to take my own personal inventory.

Dealing with Our Own Sins

Thinking this morning about how easy it is to get zealous about how someone else needs to stop living in their sin. But i am responsible to be sensitive to the Holy Spirit's conviction in my heart and obedient to God's Word, myself. God is forgiving and merciful, but He is going to deal with my sin. Because just like a parent does their best to keep their children from harm, God wants to protect us from the harm that our sin brings into our lives. Even the things we might consider little sins are harmful...things like worrying, or a bad attitude, or stressing...they are still sins of not trusting, or not resting, or not seeking God's will. I am just thinking that it is important not to get so distracted by the obvious sin of others, that i neglect to deal with my own.

My Sin Is Never Justified

Pondering on the fact that another person's sin never justifies my own. A good example would be that the driver who cuts me off in traffic, does not justify me complaining or getting mad. Instead i should stop and thank the Lord for protecting me. Or that person who hurt my feelings, does not give me the right to talk badly about them or to be cruel in return. I need to pray for them instead. Whatever the issue, my sin is never justified or excused because someone else did something wrong. I am accountable for my own actions, thoughts, and attitudes! And i don't want there to be things that come between me and my Lord! It is not enough to just desire that; it must be my conscious goal!...

Patience/ Impatience

Soaring Like Eagles

I can't tell you how many times i have read Isaiah 40:31 in my Bible or quoted it to myself or to others. Many, many times! But as i was really thinking about the part about the eagles this morning, i had a new perspective that i hadn't really taken the time to think through before. The verse says,

"But they that wait upon the Lord shall renew their strength; they shall mount up with wings like eagles; they shall run and not be weary; and they shall walk, and not faint."

Isaiah 40:31

Well, first of all, it jumps out at me that to receive these things, first, we must *wait*...and i am pretty sure most of us do not especially enjoy waiting for too much of anything. But this is waiting on the Lord! Remembering His perfect purpose, His perfect timing, and His perfect ways...So, when i am waiting on the Lord, i will soar like the eagles... When an eagle soars, it is above it all! How amazing to think that when i am willing to wait (best when i am *trusting,* and *hoping,* and *resting* in the Lord), He allows me to rise above the problems or the cares that seem to overwhelm me. Wouldn't i much rather wait on His perfect will and way, and "soar above things" that otherwise encumber me and trip me up?! Besides that, i think of the freedom that comes in that picture!!

But then the Lord brought to mind one other thought, and that is the thought that, when an eagle soars, and you are in the close vicinity of it, you can't miss the awesomeness of that picture! It is amazing! And i then am reminded that, the trials that come my way are not always for my own refining and growth, but that, often, others who know my struggles, are watching. And what a fantastic testimony we can be to let those around us see how God helps us to soar about the difficulties of this life that require *waiting on Him.* It is not easy to wait, but waiting on the Lord and trusting Him through the process can have such blessed results!

Remember that God does not promise to remove the "obstacles," but He does promise to help us to soar like the eagles!

Impatient Much?

Thinking about how everything being an instant sort of thing these days is not always a good thing. God says i need patience. He says that sometimes waiting is part of His plan. He tells us that patience brings hope. He knows that when i wait for something, i appreciate it sooo much more! I am afraid what i see in our culture, in this day and age, is that gratitude and appreciation are fading into extinction. Things are too easy and too quick. It also means that often, we don't stop and think before we act or speak. Impatience gets so that it permeates our lives to a much greater degree than we realize. It causes me to ponder the ways that the Lord knows i need to work on surrendering to Him and being more patient. His ways are perfect and perfectly timed. I want to always be grateful for the many blessings He gives. May my impatience not get in the way.

More Focus on the Product Than the Time Frame

Pondering this morning that great things take time, a tree that is massive and amazing, took years to get that way! Priceless gems take time to mine, to chip away, and to be faceted before they become those gorgeous stones we think of. A castle takes much work, many laborers, and time to help bring it to completion. The temple that Solomon built took 7 years to complete. So, why is it that as a Christian who wants to be more like Christ, i want the product with very little process? I am thinking this morning that I need to have more patience in the process and to be more concerned about the product than the time frame.

The Benefits of Waiting

Thinking about sitting still and waiting and how bad we can be about that at times, but God says when we wait on Him, our strength is renewed! Patience, hope, and trusting, all require waiting. A raw cake or unbaked bread just doesn't have the same appeal as if one waits for them to cook. A child has to develop, learn, and grow over time. So, as i think on these things, I am inspired to wait because there really are some amazing things worth waiting for!! And besides that, often the Lord shows us His glory and power in the process!

God's Patience Should Impact Mine

Thinking that i am glad God looks at patience in a different light than most of us tend to, He doesn't see it as something to dread, but as something that He gives freely because of His amazing love for me!! So, why should i not be patient with His timing when i trust His unfailing love for me?! Then, i need to take it a step further and be thankful that He teaches me to have hope in those times when i am required to be patient. I want to see His patience and to see the patience, i need to have with situations and with others, through His perspective.

What Can I Do For Him?

Deliberately Following

As i read about the Israelites, i think of how back and forth they are. They follow God; then, they turn their backs on Him. Back and forth, back and forth...and i think, "I don't want to be like that'." I want to please my Heavenly Father, not to try His patience. But the truth is, that though i do not generally deliberately disobey Him, i can easily get distracted, if i am not careful. And that is one of those subtle things that the devil uses to get Christians down the wrong road, so to speak. And i realize that i need to give more time to thinking about how i can please the Lord. When you love someone, you want to please them. You would never go out and just buy some random gift, talk to them when you wanted something or only once a day, you work at pleasing them. So, i guess what i am saying, is that i am challenged to, instead of just doing whatever and expecting the Lord to be pleased, needing to make it a priority to please the One who has given the most for me! Undeserving though i am! I don't want to be drawn subtly down a wrong road and end up so far away from my Lord, that it takes a really long time to get back to where i belong. May He give us all hearts that are drawn to Him, and may we follow His leading!

Giving Back

Have you ever had one of those friends, who only comes to you to vent or when they need something? If you are like me, i want to be willing to be there for them, but after a while it begins to wear on me because they don't seem to ever listen or give in return. But i think that i (and maybe you, only you know) can be like that at times with the Lord. I cry out to Him because i have this burden, or that burden on my heart, or there is a need, and He wants me to. But how often do i ask Him what i can do for Him?

How can i serve you Lord?

How can i minister to someone else to show Your love to them?

How can i let Your character be seen in me?

What can i do for You?

Just as i have come to depend on His provision, on every level, i in turn need to show my love toward Him, and in a sense say, "thank you," by the way i am devoted to Him! I don't even want to think about what my life would be like apart from the Lord! So i am challenged to love Him with my whole self and show it with all that i am and do. I am so very thankful that with God, all things are possible!!

Giving

Giving comes in many different forms. You can give of your time, your efforts, your money, your emotions, your knowledge, your wisdom, and your experience (and you can probably think of many other ways). Sometimes though, the giving is not so much the hard part, as the "not receiving anything in return" can become a problem. If you are like i am, i don't necessarily give so that i can get back. But i can get a little frustrated when it seems i am putting lots of effort into someone or something, and they are always willing to receive, but then, that is where it seems to stop. And that is where the struggle begins, because instead of focusing on the fact that i am to *do all as to the Lord* (Colossians 3:17), i then start to think selfishly. However, on the flip side of it...how often do i want the Lord to "give" to me, and yet not offer anything in return? Lord, please make this better, or make them better, or you can fill in the blank. But am i giving the Lord my time, myself, *any part of me, or my day?* That is sobering! He has given so much for me!! How can i not give back to Him and to others??

What Can I Do for Him?

Thinking this morning, that instead of constantly asking God to do things for me, i need to be more mindful of what i can do for Him....after all He is God!! Doing things out of love for Him and others, singing praise to Him, giving Him glory, and honor and praise, you can add to the list, i am sure!

Taking it a step further-- God is a jealous God and rightly so! He is the only one deserving of all that i am!

Doing All for God

Thinking about how well the Lord puts the thoughts of my quiet time with the day that He knows i will be having. It has definitely been a "Monday morning" for me. But the thoughts He gave me, were to do all that i do for Him. Otherwise, they are for nothing...hmm... might be a good thing to ponder, as i let Him give me His attitude in place of mine! It really does make a difference!

Glory in God, Not Mankind

"Thus saith the Lord, Let not the wise man glory in his wisdom, neither the mighty man glory in his might, let not the rich man glory in his riches: but let him who glories glory in this, that he understands and knows me, that I am the Lord which exercises lovingkindness, judgement, and righteousness, in the earth: for in these things I delight, saith the Lord." Jeremiah 9:23-24...my confidence has to be in the Lord, not in myself!

Pure Before the Lord

"Search me Lord...," should always be my prayer. I don't want sin "just hanging out" in my life. Instead, i want to be in right standing with the Lord and to be directed in His ways! This does, however, require me listening to His Word and obeying.

"Search me, O God, and know my heart: try me and know my thoughts: and see if there be any wicked way in me, and lead me in the way everlasting."
Psalm 139:23-24

Pleasing or Wearying God

As i was reading this morning in 1 Kings, i found myself wanting to get past all the bad kings to read about a good one. And it made me wonder how God must feel at times about how His children behave/misbehave. I don't want to weary Him. Yes, He is patient and forgiving, but a parent who always has to scold or discipline a child grows weary of it after a while. It is not that He loves me based on my behavior...that couldn't be further from the truth! But when i tell Him or others that i love them, my actions need to be consistent with that. I really do want to please my Heavenly Father and to be sensitive to His direction and His voice!

Worship Can Be Done Anywhere!

Thinking this morning that i am so thankful that i don't have to be in a certain place to worship my Savior and Lord! Or to talk to Him or to confess to Him!! He is with me always and is always available!! What a blessing! Don't get me wrong-- I am not against church-- not at all! But i am so very grateful that all those hours that i am not at church during a week, I can still meet with and worship God!

Time Given to God

Thinking this morning that God deserves my efforts and "sacrifices" more than anyone or anything…but that is not always how it happens. I will give up what i want to do for my children, or my grandkids, or my spouse, or even a friend. But how often do i set aside what i want to do to take time to do what i know God wants me to do?! Food for thought…

As Loyal to God as I Am to Others?

Reading about David and Jonathan, in 1 Samuel, this morning, takes my mind to the characteristic of loyalty. And my first thought is relationships with others. We would all want to be thought of as being loyal in our relationships with others. But then my mind goes to the loyalty of God to His children. How undeserving any of us are of that! And yet He is God and will not deny His own godly character! But the challenge comes in the question, 'Am i as loyal to Him?' As loyal to Him as i am to my spouse? or my friends? or my family? Do i put as much effort into my relationship with my Heavenly Father as i do in my relationships with others?! What if He was as loyal to us as we are to Him? How would that be...Just the bit of food for thought i am chewing on today...

Faithful to Him!

God is always faithful! And those of us who belong to Him are so grateful!! But i am also challenged to be faithful to Him! Sometimes that may mean leaving my comfort zone or working hard at something. Sometimes it may mean saying no to the trivial, because i know the Lord has something else He is wanting me to do or a person He wants me to encourage. And sometimes it means just being still and spending time with Him!! Whatever it may mean on a moment by moment basis, it is my desire to be faithful to the One, who loves me more than anyone else could ever love me!!

I Belong to the Lord

I am impressed this morning, about how important it is that i remember my time is not really mine, but God's. I am here to have fellowship with Him, and to accomplish His purpose...wanting to be sensitive and purposely pliable in His hands...including how i use my time each and every day...

Goal for the day...

Jesus,

Others

and then self...

Conclusion

What Does God See?

God's Word says there is nothing hidden from Him--nothing! As i ponder this, i think about how we would never want someone to think of us as a hypocrite. So, what does God see in me? I need to be much more concerned about what He thinks than what others think.

I am both encouraged and challenged as i think about the fact that there is nothing i do that is hidden from my Lord! Encouraged because He sees those things that honor Him, even if others do not, but i am also challenged, because He doesn't miss a thing. Not the bad attitudes, or selfishness, or worry, or stress...and that should keep me in check, even if no one else does.

God sees all i do and knows the motive with which i am doing it, so what is He seeing? I am so thankful that as long as i am on this earth, He will keep working in my life! And since He sees all there is in me, who better to do the working?!

There is nothing i think or do that God does not know! Nothing! But also, because of that, i am touched by the fact that He has chosen to love me! And i am so thankful that He is refining me along the way.

Thinking about the phrase "enduring til the end"...and that it is not only about what i am doing to bring others' attention to the Lord, but it is so important to consider the attitude with which i do those things. Is it a stressful one, a caring one, one of anxiety or of peace? Is it sweet or sour? God says man looks on the outward appearance, but He looks at the heart. We can fool people sometimes, but never God! He sees me through and through. So, I trust that my goal, and yours will be to reflect Christ from the inside out."

About the Author

I must say I was blessed to be born to Christian parents. At a fairly young age, I put my faith in Jesus as my Savior. It was definitely to my benefit that my Dad was a pastor, and I grew up with lots of Biblical teaching. But truly the Lord has made me who I am. My husband and I have been married for over 34 years. In that time, we had two children, who I homeschooled through their high school graduations. In that time frame, I also babysat for others, in our home. Now I have five amazing grandchildren! At times I get the opportunity to teach ladies Bible studies (which I love). I quite enjoy writing and singing as well.

the Butterfly Typeface